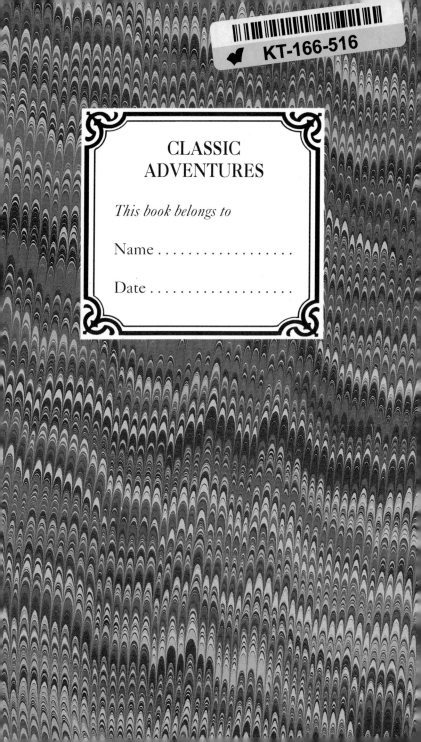

CLASSIC ADVENTURES

This book belongs to

Name . . . .

Date . . . .

Heidi

Heidi

By
Johanna Spyri

The Classic Adventures Series

First published by Collins
This facsimile edition
© Fabbri Publishing Ltd 1990
Printed and bound in Spain by Printer
Industria Gráfica, Barcelona

ISBN 1-85587-306-0

Contents

Contents

CHAPTER 1

Up to the Alm-Uncle

~~~~~~~~

From the old and pleasantly situated town of Maienfeld a path leads through green, shady meadows to the foot of the mountains which look down from their majestic heights upon the valley below. As the footpath begins to slope gently upwards, the fragrance of the nearby heath, with its short grass and vigorous mountain plants, fills the air; then the way becomes more rugged and the path rises steeply towards the Alps.

One bright, sunny morning in June, a tall, sturdy-looking girl of this mountainous country climbed the narrow mountain path, leading a child by the hand. The little girl's cheeks were aglow and the bright crimson shone even through her brown, sunburnt skin. This was not surprising, for in spite of the scorching sun the child was wrapped up as though for protection against bitter frost. She wore two, if not three frocks, one on top of the other, and, in addition, a big red shawl was tied all round her body so that her little five-year-old figure was scarcely discernible. In her heavy, nailed mountain shoes, she toiled laboriously up the slope. The two figures had been climbing from the valley for about an hour when they reached the hamlet called Dorfli which is situated half-way up the Alm. Here they were greeted with friendly calls from every doorway, for this was the girl's birthplace. But she hurried on until she had reached the last of the scattered little houses, and as she passed, a

1

voice called from the doorway, " Wait for me, Dete, if you are going up and I will come, too ! "

She stood still. A stout, kind-looking woman came out of the house and joined them. " Where are you taking the child, Dete?" she asked. "I suppose it is your sister's child—the orphan?"

"Yes," answered Dete. "I am taking her to stay with the Alm-Uncle."

"Surely you aren't going to leave the child with *him*. You must be out of your mind, Dete! But the old man is sure to turn you away, in any case!"

"He can't do that! He is her grandfather. I have looked after the child up till now, and I can tell you, Barbel, I am not going to turn down the offer of a good job on her account. From now on the grandfather will have to do his bit."

"Oh, well, if he were like other people——" replied Barbel, "but you know him as well as I do. How can he look after a child, and especially such a little one? Oh, she will never stay with him! But where are *you* going, Dete?"

"To a very good job in Frankfurt," explained Dete.

"Well, I wouldn't like to be the child," said Barbel disapprovingly. "Nobody knows anything about the old man up there. He never speaks to anybody. With his bushy eyebrows and terrible beard he looks a positive savage. The whole village is afraid of him."

"Still," Dete persisted, " he is the grandfather and it's up to him to look after the child."

"They say all sorts of terrible things about the old man," said Barbel, glancing keenly at her companion. "You must surely have heard his history from your sister, eh, Dete ? "

"Perhaps I have, but I shan't say. It would be a fine thing for me if he found out I had been talking ! "

Barbel had been eager for a long time to learn something about the old man whom everybody referred to as the Alm-Uncle. She wanted to know why he seemed to hate everybody and why he lived all by himself up on the mountain. Confidentially she took Dete's arm. "Do tell me, now! You have nothing to fear," she coaxed.

Dete looked round to see whether the child were nearby and might hear what she had to say, but the little one was not in sight. Dete stopped in some consternation, and looked back. There was no sign of the child.

"Now I see her!" cried Barbel at last. "Over there!" She pointed far away from the path. "She is climbing the slopes with Peter, the goat-herd, and his goats. He can look after the child, and you will be able to go on with your story."

"She's good enough at looking after herself," said Dete, " and perhaps it's a good thing, for the old man will not be able to provide for her very well. He has nothing now but his two goats and the Alm cottage."

"Did he have more in his younger days?" asked Barbel.

"Yes, I should think he did!" replied Dete with conviction. "He was brought up on one of the finest farms in Domleschg. He was the eldest son. But he lost the farm with his gambling and drinking, and, when the whole story of his wild extravagance came out, his parents died of grief. He disappeared after that and at first nobody knew where he had gone. Some said he joined the army in Naples. No more news came for about twelve to fifteen years. Then, suddenly, he appeared again in Domleschg with an almost grown-up boy and tried to find a home for him with relations. But every door was closed against him.

"That so embittered him that he vowed he would never again set foot in Domleschg and came with the boy to Dorfli to live. It seems he still had a little money left—enough for the boy, Tobias, to be apprenticed to a carpenter. He was a good boy and well liked by everyone in Dorfli. But nobody trusted the old man. There was a rumour that he had to get out of Naples to avoid serious trouble, because it was said that he had killed a man—of course, not in the war, you understand, but in some brawl. But we did not break our connection with him since we were closely related. We called him 'Uncle,' and as we are related on my father's side to almost everybody in Dorfli, the whole village called him 'Uncle,' too. And because he lived on the Alm he was called the 'Alm-Uncle.'"

"But what happened to Tobias?" asked Barbel eagerly.

"Well, Tobias served his apprenticeship in Mels, and as soon as he had finished he came home to Dorfli and married my sister, Adelheid. They were very happy together, but their happiness was short-lived. Two years later, while Tobias was working at the building of a house, a beam fell on him and killed him, and when his mutilated body was brought home Adelheid fell into a violent fever as a result of the shock, and never recovered. In any case, she was not very strong and sometimes took strange fits when we couldn't tell whether she was asleep or awake.

"Only a few weeks after Tobias died, Adelheid too was buried. Some said it was the uncle's punishment for the wicked life he had led, and they even told him so to his face. The pastor, too, begged him to repent of his past sins but the uncle only grew more fierce and embittered. Then we heard he had come to live on the Alm and he has remained up there in solitude ever since, at war with God and the world.

"Mother and I took in Adelheid's little child. She was only a year old then. When Mother died last summer and I had to go and work at the health resort, I took the child with me and left her in charge of old Ursel up in Pfaferserdorf. I was kept on at the health resort during the winter, and early in the spring some Frankfurt people I had served during the summer came back. They offered me a job, and I am going away with them to Frankfurt. We leave the day after to-morrow."

"And you are going to leave the poor child with that terrible old man!" said Barbel reproachfully.

"Well, what else can I do?" replied Dete defensively. "I can't take her with me. But, goodness! Where are you going, Barbel? We are already half-way up the Alm."

"I have almost come as far as I need," answered Barbel. "I want to speak to Peter's grandmother. She spins for me in winter. Good-bye, then, Dete! And good luck!"

Dete shook her friend's hand and stopped while Barbel walked towards the little brown Alm hut which was situated in a sheltered spot some yards off the path. The hut was more than half-way up the Alm from the village. It was fortunate it stood in such a sheltered place, for it looked dilapidated beyond repair. Even situated as it was, it was hardly safe to live in when gales swept the mountains. Then everything in the hut, doors and windows and all the old beams, would shake and crack.

The goat-herd lived here with his mother and his old blind grandmother. Peter was eleven years old. Every morning he collected goats from the village and drove them up to the Alm where they grazed till evening.

Dete stood looking impatiently in all directions to catch a glimpse of the children and the goats; but they had taken a very roundabout way. At first the little girl had toiled hard to climb with the goat-herd, panting in the heat and making a great effort under her heavy encumbrance of clothes. She did not say a word but looked steadily, now at Peter who jumped about on his bare feet, now at the goats who climbed still more easily on their slender little legs. Suddenly the child sat down on the ground and quickly removed her shoes and stockings. Then, standing up, she began to take off her many layers of clothing until, clad only in her light little petticoat, she stood with her little bare arms stretched happily into the air. Then she put everything neatly into a little pile and jumped and climbed behind the goats. As she came skipping along in her new garb, Peter grinned broadly. He looked back, and when he saw the little pile of clothes lying on the path he grinned even more, but he said nothing. The child, feeling free at last, began to chatter to the boy, asking him how many goats he had, where he was going with them and what he would do there. So at last the children arrived at the cottage and caught sight of Aunt Dete. She no sooner spotted the group than she cried, "Heidi! What a sight you are! Where are your clothes? And the new shoes I bought you, and the stockings I knitted? Where have you put them?"

The child quietly pointed down the hill.

The aunt followed the direction of her finger. There was, indeed, something lying on the ground. "You dreadful child!" she cried in great annoyance. "What's the meaning of this? Why have you taken everything off?"

"I didn't need them," said the child, not looking at all penitent.

"Oh, have you no sense?" lamented the aunt. "Who is to go back down for them?" Then turning to Peter, she ordered, "Peter! Run back and fetch the clothes!"

"I am late already," said Peter slowly, and remained motionless, both hands in his pockets.

"Don't just stand there staring!" Aunt Dete cried. "This will never do! Come here! I will give you something good. Look!" And she held up a bright new coin. The boy's eyes shone at the sight of it. Suddenly he jumped up and made off down the Alm by the shortest way. Soon he reached the little pile of clothes, gathered them up and sped back so quickly that the aunt could not but be pleased, and at once gave him the coin. Peter put it in his pocket, his face wreathed in smiles.

"You can take the clothes up to the uncle's since you are going that way," Aunt Dete said as she started to climb the steep slope which rose just behind Goat Peter's cottage. Readily Peter carried out the order and followed as she walked ahead; his left arm round the bundle, the goats' stick swinging in his right hand. Heidi and the goats leaped joyously at his side. Thus, in three quarters of an hour, the little group reached the top of the Alm where the old uncle's cottage stood on a ledge of the mountain. Along the side of the cottage facing the valley, the uncle had made himself a bench, and here he now sat puffing his pipe, both hands on his knees, calmly watching the children, the goats and Aunt Dete as they climbed. Heidi arrived first. She went straight up to the old man, stretched out her hand towards him and said, "Good evening, Grandfather!"

"Well, well! What is the meaning of this?" asked the old man gruffly. He took the child's hand abruptly and as he did so a long, piercing glance shot from beneath his bushy eyebrows. Heidi returned his look without blinking.

In the meantime, the aunt and Peter had arrived.

"I wish you good day!" said Dete shortly. "This is Tobias' and Adelheid's child. You will hardly recognise her because you have not seen her since she was a year old."

"What have I to do with the child?" asked the old man brusquely. "And you, there!" he called to Peter.

"Take yourself off with your goats! You are late as it is."

Peter obeyed at once, for the uncle had given him an angry look which did not make him wish to linger.

"The child just has to stay with you, Uncle," said Dete. "I have done my bit for four years. Now it is your turn."

"Indeed!" mumbled the old man, his glance flashing at Dete. "And if the child starts fretting for you what shall I do with her then?"

"That's up to you," replied Dete. "No one told me what to do with the little one when she was left in my care, and only one year old, too. Now I have to make my own living and you are the child's nearest relative. If you can't look after her it's your responsibility and you must answer for any harm that comes to her. And I shouldn't think you can afford to add another to your list of wicked deeds."

At her last words, the old man got up. He looked so threatening that she took a step backwards. Flinging out his arm, he shouted at her, "Be off! And don't be in a hurry to show your face here again!"

Dete did not need a second telling. "Good-bye, then!" she said hurriedly. "And you, too, Heidi!" And with that she turned and ran all the way back to Dorfli.

This time, people were even more eager to stop and question her, wondering what had become of the child. They all knew Dete well, and also the history of the child. When voices called from every door and window, "Where is the child, Dete? What have you done with her?" she replied angrily, "With the Alm-Uncle, of course! I left her with the Alm-Uncle, just as I said."

Dete ran through the village as fast as she could go. Her one thought was to get away from Dorfli and to avoid speaking to any one, for she was far from easy in her conscience about what she had done.

CHAPTER 2

The Grandfather's Hut

◆◆◆◆◆◆◆

Long after Dete had gone, the grandfather sat silently blowing clouds of smoke from his pipe while Heidi began to inspect her new surroundings. She peeped into the goat-house and then walked round to the other side of the cottage where there stood three old fir trees. A strong wind shook their thick branches and the child stood still, listening to the moaning of the wind in the ancient trees. Then she completed the circuit of the cottage and returned to where the grandfather sat. She went across and stood in front of him, her hands clasped behind her back, her steady eyes looking at him.

The old man raised his head. "Well, what are we going to do now?"

"I would like to see inside the cottage."

"Come, then!" The grandfather got up. "And bring your bundle of clothes!"

"I don't need them any more," declared Heidi.

The old man turned and looked searchingly at the child. "She doesn't lack sense, anyway," he said quietly to himself. Then, "Why don't you need them any more?" he asked aloud.

"I would rather be dressed like the goats with their bare legs."

"All right, then, but bring the things!" commanded the grandfather. "We will put them in the cupboard."

Heidi obediently picked up her bundle and followed the old man inside. The door opened directly on to a

9

big room which was the full breadth of the cottage. The only furniture in the room was a table and a chair. In one corner stood the grandfather's bed and in the opposite wall was the fireplace above which hung a big kettle. On the same side as the bed, in the middle of the wall, there was a door which the grandfather now opened. This was the cupboard where he kept his belongings. On a shelf lay a couple of shirts, socks and some rough sack-cloth sheets. On another stood plates, cups and glasses, and on the top shelf there was a round loaf, a sausage, ham and cheese. As soon as the door was opened Heidi came forward and pushed her own clothes as far behind the grandfather's as possible so that they would be well out of the way. Then she turned her attention to the room and asked, "Where shall I sleep, Grandfather?"

"Wherever you want to."

This seemed to please the child and she began to inspect every corner. By the grandfather's bed, wooden steps went up, and when the child climbed the little ladder she found herself in the hay-loft. A bale of hay, fresh and sweet-smelling, lay on the floor, and from a little window in the roof she could see far down into the valley.

"Oh, this is where I want to sleep!" she cried joyfully. "It is lovely! Come and see how lovely it is, Grandfather!"

"I have seen it before!" came from below.

"I am going to make my bed," the child called again and ran busily to and fro. "You must bring me a sheet, Grandfather!"

"Indeed!" remarked the grandfather, and after a while he went to the cupboard and raked about amongst the clothes. Presently he pulled out a long, coarse piece of sack-cloth which might serve as a sheet. He carried it up to the loft and there he saw that a very nice little bed had been made amongst the hay, with extra hay piled up into a pillow at one end, and arranged in such a way that whoever lay on the improvised bed would be able to look up at the little window.

"Well done!" exclaimed the grandfather. "Now the sheet goes on. But wait——!" and here he took a big bunch of hay and made the bed twice as thick so that the hardness of the floor would not come through.

"Now bring it here!"

Heidi quickly grasped the sheet but it was so thick and heavy, she staggered under the weight. Together they spread the sheet and now the bed looked very trim and tidy; but Heidi stood back and regarded it critically.

"There is still something we have forgotten, Grandfather."

"Now what?" he asked.

"A top sheet."

"Oh, indeed! But what if I haven't got any?"

"Don't worry, Grandfather," Heidi consoled him. "We can use more hay for a cover," and she began to gather another bundle.

"Wait a moment!" The old man went down the steps to his own bed. Back he came presently with a big, heavy, linen sack which he laid on the floor.

"Isn't that better than hay?" he asked, helping her to spread it on the bed.

Heidi stood admiringly before her new sleeping-place. "The cover is beautiful!" she declared ecstatically, "and the bed is just perfect! I wish it were night-time already so that I could go to sleep on it!"

"I think we should eat first," the grandfather advised.

In her eagerness, Heidi had forgotten everything except the new bed, but now, when she thought of it, she did indeed feel very hungry, for she had had nothing to eat since morning. "Yes, I think so, too!" she agreed.

"Well, then, since we are in such complete agreement, let's go down," said the old man, guiding the child towards the stairs.

In the room below he went over to the fireplace, pushed back the big kettle and brought a little one forward on the chain. Then he sat down on a three-legged stool and blew up the fire. It was soon blazing merrily and the little kettle began to boil. Next the old man cut a big piece of cheese, and piercing it with a long, iron fork, he held it over the fire, turning it constantly to and fro until it was golden brown all over. Heidi had watched all these operations with the closest attention and apparently some new ideas had entered her head for suddenly she jumped up and went to the cupboard. When the grandfather had decided that the cheese was nicely toasted and took it to the table, there was the round loaf, two plates and two knives neatly laid, for Heidi had been quick to see what was wanted and had brought everything from the cupboard.

"So you can think for yourself! That's good!" said the grandfather and spread the toasted cheese on the bread. "But there is still something missing."

Heidi's eyes alighted on the steaming pot by the fire and she knew at once what it was. Quickly she ran back to the cupboard but could find only one little bowl. She hesitated only a moment for right at the back were two glasses. Presently she came back and put the little bowl and a glass on the table.

"Very good! Very good!" said the old man. "You have found a way out of the difficulty. But now, where are *you* going to sit?" and he drew his own chair up to the table.

Heidi ran to the hearth and brought back the little three-legged stool.

"You have got a seat, at any rate," said the grandfather, "though it is rather low! Even on my chair you would be too small to reach the table. But now you must eat. Come along!"

He filled the little bowl with milk and placing it on his own chair pushed it near the stool so that Heidi had a little table of her own. Then he filled a plate with a big piece of bread and some of the yellow, toasted cheese and laid it also on the chair. He himself sat on the corner of the table and began his meal. Heidi lifted her little bowl and drank without stopping.

"Do you like the milk?" the grandfather asked.

"It is the best milk I have ever tasted!" replied Heidi.

"You can have more," said the grandfather, filling the little bowl again and putting it before her.

The cheese was soft as butter and tasted good. From time to time Heidi took a drink from the bowl and looked blissfully happy.

When the meal was finished, the grandfather went out to the goat-house where there was work to be done. Heidi watched him attentively, observing how he first swept everything clean with the broom then spread fresh straw for the little animals to sleep on. At last the goat-house was finished and he went into the shed which was close by. Here he chopped several round sticks to equal lengths; then he carefully shaped a flat piece of wood and drilled four holes into one side. He put the round sticks into the holes—and there was a chair like the grandfather's, only much higher! Speechless with admiration, Heidi gazed at it.

"What do you think it is, Heidi?" asked the grandfather.

"It is *my* chair, because it is so high."

"She has eyes in her head all right," thought the grandfather as he walked round the cottage, fixing a loose board at the door and repairing anything that needed attention. Heidi followed close behind. Nothing escaped her notice.

Evening came, and the old fir trees behind the cottage began to rustle more loudly as a strong wind swept along, roaring amongst the branches. Heidi's heart beat faster. She thought she had never heard anything so beautiful and went skipping and running for sheer joy under the trees. All the while the grandfather watched the child from the doorway.

There was the sound of a shrill whistle. Heidi stood still and the grandfather stepped out of the cottage. From above, the goats came jumping like wild creatures and in the midst of them was Peter. With a joyful cry, Heidi rushed to welcome her old friends of the morning. At the cottage, children and animals came to a halt and two pretty, slender goats, one brown, one white, ran from the herd towards the grandfather. Eagerly they licked his hands for in the palms he held a little salt which the goats liked very much. Peter disappeared with the rest of the flock and Heidi fell to caressing first one and then the other of the goats and jumped gaily round them.

"Do they belong to us, Grandfather? Do they really belong to us?" she asked. "Will they stay in the little shed? Do they always stay with us?" Heidi scarcely gave the grandfather a chance to put in his steady, "Yes! Yes!" between one question and the next.

When the goats had finished licking the salt from his hands, the old man commanded, "Go fetch your little bowl and the bread!"

Heidi obeyed at once. Then the grandfather milked the white goat into the little bowl which was soon full to the brim. He cut a piece of bread and handing it to the child said, "Eat now, and then go upstairs to sleep. I suppose your night things are in the bundle Aunt Dete made up. Get it out if you need it. I have to tie up the goats for the night. Sleep well!"

"Good night, Grandfather! But what are the goats' names? Tell me, Grandfather!" cried the child, running behind the old man's receding figure.

"The white one is called 'Little Swan' and the brown one is 'Little Bear,'" the grandfather called over his shoulder.

"Good night, Little Swan! Good night, Little Bear!" cried Heidi happily as all three disappeared into the goat-house.

Heidi went back to the bench outside the cottage where she sat and took her bread and milk. The wind was so strong she was almost blown from her seat, so she finished hurriedly and went into the house and upstairs to bed where she was soon fast asleep, as soundly and happily as though on the best feather-bed. Not long after, and before the darkness had come completely, the grandfather, too, had gone to bed, for he always rose at sunrise. All night long the wind blew strongly so that the whole cottage seemed to shake and every beam cracked and groaned.

In the middle of the night the grandfather rose, saying half aloud to himself, "Perhaps she is afraid." He climbed the steps and stood by Heidi's bed. At intervals the moon shone brightly, then as clouds were chased across it everything became dark again. At that moment a shaft of moonlight came through the little window, falling directly on Heidi's bed. Her cheeks were flushed from sleep and her head rested quietly and peacefully on her little round arms. Her dreams appeared to be happy ones for a smile played about her mouth. The grandfather gazed at the sleeping child until the moon was again overshadowed. Then he turned away in the darkness and went back to his bed.

CHAPTER 3

On the Alm

━━━━━━━

ARLY IN THE morning, Heidi was awakened by a loud whistle. As she opened her eyes, a gleam of sunshine came through the little window on to her bed and shone on the hay nearby so that everything was bathed in golden light. Heidi looked puzzled and tried to think where she was. Then, from outside, she heard the grandfather's deep, quiet voice and she remembered that she was up on the Alm. She no longer lived with old Ursel who was almost stone deaf and always wanted to have Heidi by her side, so that sometimes the child had felt like a prisoner and would have liked to run away. So she was very glad when she awoke and found herself in her new home. She remembered all the exciting things she had seen the previous day and wondered what this new day had in store for her. Above all she looked forward to seeing Little Swan and Little Bear again. Quickly she jumped out of bed and in a few minutes had dressed herself. Then she climbed down the steps and ran out to the front of the cottage. Peter, the goat-herd, was already there with his flock and the grandfather was leading out Little Swan and Little Bear to join them. Heidi ran forward to say good-morning to him and the goats.

"How would you like to go with them to the pasture?" asked the grandfather.

Heidi was overjoyed. That was the thing she would like best of all.

"But first you must wash yourself or the sun, shining

brightly up there, will laugh at you when he looks down and sees how dirty you are! See! This is where you wash." The grandfather pointed towards a big flat tub filled with water which stood in the sun before the cottage door. Heidi jumped towards it and splashed and scrubbed until she was perfectly clean. In the meantime the grandfather went into the cottage, calling to Peter, "Come here, goat-general, and bring your rucksack!"

Amazed, Peter answered the call and laid down the rucksack in which he carried his meagre lunch.

"Open it!" ordered the old man, and then put in a big piece of bread and an equally big piece of cheese. Peter opened his round eyes very wide for this food was twice as much as he had for his own lunch.

"And now the little bowl has to go in, too," the old man continued. "At lunch-time you will milk for her two little bowlfuls, for she is going, too, and can stay with you until you come back in the evening. Take care she doesn't fall over the precipice!"

Now Heidi came running towards them. "Grand-father, the sun can't laugh at me now!" For fear of the sun's mockery she had rubbed her face, neck and arms so vigorously with the rough cloth which the grandfather had hung up beside the water-tub, that she was almost as red as a lobster.

The old man smiled. "No, he has no reason to laugh now," he agreed. "But do you know what happens when you come home in the evening? You go right into the tub like a fish because if you run like the goats your feet will get dirty. Now, off you go!"

Happily the children climbed up the Alm. The high winds during the night had blown away the last little cloud and now the sky was a vast expanse of deep blue out of which the sun shone and glittered on the green slopes. The little blue and yellow mountain flowers opened their cups and seemed to nod merrily at Heidi who romped everywhere. Enchanted by this sparkling, waving sea of flowers, she forgot all about Peter, even about the goats. All along the way she picked flowers until she had a big bunch which she wrapped in her pinafore, for she wanted to take them home.

Peter was quite dazed trying to look in every direction at once, for the goats, like Heidi, were jumping from one place to another. He had to whistle and shout and brandish his stick to bring the goats together again.

"Where are you now, Heidi?" came the boy's exasperated and rather angry cry.

"Here!" came the reply, but Peter could see no one. Heidi was sitting, hidden from view, behind a little hillock.

"Come here!" Peter called again. "You are not to go near the precipice—the uncle said so!"

"Where is that?" asked Heidi, still not moving from her hiding-place.

"Up there! Right on the top the old eagle sits on the look-out for his prey."

That did the trick.

At once Heidi jumped up and ran to Peter with her apronful of flowers.

"That is enough flower-picking for now," he said as they climbed up together, "if you are going to keep pace with me. And if you pick all the flowers to-day there will be none left for to-morrow."

Heidi was convinced. Moreover, her pinafore was so full that it could hardly hold another one. So she now walked quietly beside Peter. The pasture which Peter usually chose and where he spent the day was situated at the foot of the high rocks. Bushes and fir trees covered the lower parts but nearer the summit the rocks rose bare and rugged towards the sky. On one side of the mountain, jagged clefts stretched far down and the grandfather had been right to warn Peter of the danger. When they had reached the pasture, Peter carefully put his rucksack into a little hollow in the ground, for the wind often blew with great violence across this part of the country and Peter did not want to see his precious possessions rolling down the mountainside. Then the boy, tired after the strenuous climb, stretched himself out at full length on the sunny pasture.

Heidi, by this time, had undone her pinafore and rolled it neatly round the flowers which she laid beside Peter's rucksack in the hollow. Then she sat down beside him and looked around. The valley lay far below, bathed in the sparkling morning sunshine. In front of Heidi a big, broad snowfield rose up to the dark blue sky and on the left stood a huge pile of rocks above which a bare rocky peak reached towards the sky, towering majestically above the child. Heidi sat motionless. A great silence was all around and only the delicate blue harebells and yellow cistus swayed softly in the gentle breeze, nodding joyfully on their slender little stems. Peter had fallen asleep and the goats were climbing high up amongst the bushes. Heidi had never been so happy. The golden sunlight, the fresh breezes and the delicate perfume of the flowers filled her with delight and she only wished that she might stay there for ever. She gazed so long at the mountains that it seemed to her that each had a face and that these mountain-faces were as familiar to her as old friends.

Suddenly Heidi heard a loud, harsh cry and when she looked up she saw, circling overhead, a huge bird, larger than she had ever seen before. His large wings were outspread and he flew in a wide circle, coming back again and again and uttering loud, piercing shrieks above Heidi's head.

"Peter! Peter! Wake up!" cried Heidi. "Look! There is a big bird just above us!"

Peter got up and watched the bird, too, as it rose higher and higher and at last disappeared behind the grey rocks.

"Where has he gone to?" asked Heidi who had been watching the bird with keen interest.

"Home to his nest," replied Peter.

"Is his home up there? Oh, how nice to live so high up! How terribly he cries! Let's climb up there and see where his nest is!"

"Oh, no!" replied Peter emphatically. "Even the goats can't climb so high and the uncle said you were not to climb the rocks."

Suddenly Peter started to whistle and call loudly. Heidi could not think what this meant, but the goats apparently understood, for, one after another, they came springing down until they were all gathered together on the green slope. Some continued to nibble and others ran about, playfully pushing each other with their horns. Heidi jumped up and ran amongst them. While she played with the goats Peter fetched the rucksack and laid out the four pieces of bread on the ground, the big ones on Heidi's side and the small ones on his own. Then he took the little bowl, drew some milk into it from Little Swan and placed it in the centre. " Stop skipping now! It is time to eat," he said.

Heidi sat down. "Is the milk for me?" she asked.

"Yes," replied Peter, "and the two big pieces of bread and cheese are yours too, and when you have finished you get another bowlful from Little Swan."

Heidi began to drink her milk and as soon as she put down her empty bowl Peter filled it again. Then Heidi gave a big piece of her bread to Peter and all the cheese as well, saying, "You can have it all. I have had enough."

Peter gazed at her, speechless with surprise. Never in his life could he have given away as much as that. He hesitated a little, for he could not believe that Heidi meant it seriously. She held out the pieces, but as Peter still did not take them she laid the food on his knees. Peter had never before had such a satisfying lunch.

The animals had begun to climb up again towards the bushes; some skipping gaily over everything, others stopping to taste the tender herbs.

"Peter," Heidi said presently, "the prettiest of all are Little Swan and Little Bear."

"I know," Peter replied. "The uncle brushes and washes them, and gives them salt, and has the nicest shed."

Suddenly Peter jumped up and bounded after the goats. Heidi followed. Something must have happened and she simply could not stay behind. Peter forced his way through the middle of the herd to that side of the Alm where the bare and jagged rocks fell away steeply. Here, a heedless little goat might easily tumble down and break his legs. Peter had noticed inquisitive little Goldfinch jumping in that direction. The boy arrived just in time, for the little goat was just about to jump towards the edge of the precipice. Peter, lunging towards the goat fell down and only managed to seize one of its legs as he fell. Goldfinch gave an angry cry at finding herself caught and tried desperately to free herself. Peter could not get up and shouted for Heidi to help because he was afraid Goldfinch might wrench her leg. Heidi was already there and at once saw the danger. She quickly gathered some sweet-smelling plants from the ground and held them out towards Goldfinch, saying coaxingly, "Come along, Goldfinch, and be good! Look! You might fall down and hurt yourself."

The little goat turned quickly and ate the herbs

from Heidi's outstretched hand. In the meantime Peter
got to his feet again and held Goldfinch by the cord
with which her little bell was fastened to her neck.
Heidi grasped the goat in the same way at the other side
of its head and together they led the truant back to the
peacefully grazing flock. As soon as Peter got her back
to safety, he raised his stick and started to give her a
good beating. Goldfinch, however, knowing what was
in store, timidly shrank back, and Heidi cried, "No,
Peter! No! You mustn't beat her! Look how frightened
she is!"

"She deserves it," Peter muttered, about to strike; but
Heidi threw herself against his arm, crying indignantly,
"Don't touch her! You will hurt her! Leave her alone!"

Peter turned surprised eyes on the fierce little girl
and his stick dropped to his side. "All right, then, I'll
let her off—if you give me some of your cheese to-morrow
again," he bargained.

"You can have it all, to-morrow and every day. I
don't want it," Heidi consented. "And I'll give you the
bread, too, the same as to-day, but you must promise
never to beat Goldfinch or Snowflake, or any of the
goats."

"Suits me," said Peter, and that was as good as a
promise. He let Goldfinch go and the little goat leapt
joyously towards the herd.

So the day passed quickly and the sun began to sink
behind the mountains. Heidi was sitting quietly on the
ground, gazing at the cistus and the harebells which
glistened in the evening sunshine ; rocks and grass
shimmered in a golden glow. Suddenly she jumped up
and cried, "Peter! Peter! They are on fire! They are all
on fire! All the mountains are burning! And the great
snow mountain also, and the sky! Oh, look at the lovely
fiery snow! Peter, get up and look! The fire is at the

great bird's nest, too. Look at the rocks and the fir trees! Everything is on fire!"

"It is always like that," replied Peter with great unconcern, continuing to peel his stick, "but it is not real fire."

"What is it, then?" asked Heidi, gazing eagerly around. "What is it, Peter?"

"It just gets like that," Peter tried to explain.

"Oh, look, look, Peter!" cried Heidi again in great excitement. "Everything is turning a rosy pink colour. Look at the snow and the high rocks! What are their names Peter?"

"Mountains don't have names," replied Peter.

"Oh, how beautiful! Crimson snow! Oh, now all the rocks are turning grey—now the colour is all gone. Now it is all over, Peter."

Heidi sat down, looking as distressed as if everything really had come to an end.

"To-morrow it will be the same," said Peter. "Get up now. We must go home."

"Will it be like this every day we are on the pasture?" asked Heidi insistently, as she walked down the Alm at Peter's side.

"Mostly," he replied.

Heidi was very happy. She had absorbed so many new impressions . . . had so many new things to think about that she was quite silent until they reached the hut and saw the grandfather sitting on the bench under the fir trees. Here he sat in the evenings, waiting for his goats.

Heidi ran up to him, followed by Little Swan and Little Bear, for the goats knew their master.

"Good night!" Peter called after Heidi, and then added, "Come again, to-morrow!" because he was very anxious for her to go with him.

Heidi raced towards the old man.

"Oh, Grandfather, it was wonderful!" she cried long before she reached him. "The fire on the snow and the rocks and the blue and yellow flowers, and look what I have brought for you!" Heidi unfolded her pinafore and all the flowers fell at the grandfather's feet. But what a sight the poor flowers were! Heidi did not recognise them. They were like withered grass and not a single little cup was open. "Grandfather, what is the matter with the flowers?" cried Heidi, quite alarmed. "They weren't like that before. What is wrong with them?"

"They would rather be out in the sun than tied up in a pinafore," explained the grandfather.

"Then I will never gather any more. But Grandfather, why did the eagle screech so?" Heidi asked.

"You had better have your bath now," said the grandfather, "and I shall fetch some milk from the shed. Afterwards, when we are having our supper you can tell me about everything."

Later, when Heidi sat in her high chair, the little bowl of milk in front of her and the grandfather at her side, she again asked her question.

"Why did the great bird scream at us, Grandfather?"

"He screams in mockery of the people in the villages down in the valley where they sit gossiping together. He wants to say, ' If you would all mind your own business or climb up into the heights like me you would be much happier! '"

The grandfather spoke these words with such vehemence that Heidi seemed to hear again the croaking of the great bird.

"Why don't the mountains have names, Grandfather?" asked Heidi again.

"They have names," he answered, "and if you can

describe one to me so that I can recognise it, then I will tell you its name."

Heidi tried to describe the rocky mountain with the two high peaks exactly as she had seen it. Presently the grandfather interrupted, "Yes, I know that one. Its name is Falknis. Did you notice any others?"

Then Heidi recalled the mountain with the large snowfield which looked at first as if it were on fire and then turned rose-coloured, then pale pink, and at last faded back to its own grey colour.

"I know that one, too," said the grandfather. "That is the Scesaplana. Did you like being on the pasture?"

Now Heidi told him everything: how wonderful it had been and particularly about the fire in the evening. Heidi wanted the grandfather to explain why this had happened, since Peter had been unable to do so.

"You see," the grandfather instructed her, "that's what the sun does when he says good night to the mountains. He throws his most beautiful rays over them so that they won't forget him before morning."

Heidi was delighted. She could hardly wait for the next day when she would again be allowed to go to the pasture, to watch how the sun said good night to the mountains. But first she had to go to bed, and how soundly she slept all night on her hay bed and dreamt of nothing but glistening mountains tinged with red, and Little Snowflake running happily about!

CHAPTER 4

Peter's Grandmother

~~~~~~~~

NEXT MORNING, the sun shone brightly as Peter appeared with the goats and they all went up together to the pasture. And so it continued every day. Heidi grew stronger and sturdier with living so much in the open and her little sunburnt face shone with health. When autumn came and the wind blew with greater force over the mountains, the grandfather would sometimes say, "To-day you had better stay at home, Heidi. A little one like you might easily be swept down the mountainside by the wind."

But when Peter heard this in the morning he would look very miserable. He found it dull now without Heidi; and, of course, he got less to eat. On such days the goats would become so stubborn that he had twice as much trouble with them. They, too, had grown so accustomed to Heidi that they would hardly move off without her.

Heidi herself was never bored because she always saw something new and exciting to take up her attention. Best of all she liked to go up the Alm with the goats but she also liked to watch the grandfather at work, helping him all she could at the carpenter's bench.

Then a very special treat for Heidi was to watch the grandfather prepare the lovely round goat's milk cheese. But even in the midst of such exciting activities she would sometimes steal away when the wind blew strongest to stand and listen beneath the old fir trees, catching her breath as the wind roared amongst the branches.

As the season changed, the sun lost the fierce heat of summer and Heidi looked out her warm stockings and shoes and her wool dress. Gradually the weather grew colder and Peter would appear early in the morning blowing on his hands to warm them. Then one morning they awoke to find the whole Alm covered in snow. Not one blade of grass was visible. Peter and the goats did not appear and Heidi watched from the window of the hut as the big snowflakes fell. The snow fell thickly until it reached above the window so that it was impossible to open it and Heidi and the Alm-Uncle were imprisoned in the hut. This amused Heidi and she ran from one window to another expecting the hut to be covered right over at any moment. The next day it had stopped snowing and the grandfather forced his way out and shovelled the snow away from around the hut. Soon the snow was heaped up around the cottage and they were able to open the window again. In the afternoon, as Heidi and the grandfather sat together by the fire there came a great thumping outside the door. At last the door opened and there stood Peter, knocking the snow from his boots.

"Good evening!" he said coming in and at once getting as near as possible to the fire. After this salutation the boy lapsed into silence but his whole face beamed with joy.

Heidi looked at him in amazement for the snow which had covered him from head to foot was beginning to melt and ran from him in rivulets.

"Well, General, and how are things going?" called the grandfather. "Now that the goat army has been disbanded you will have to turn to nibbling at the slate pencil."

"Why must he nibble the slate pencil?" asked Heidi at once.

"In winter the boy has to go to school," explained the grandfather. "There he learns to read and write and that is sometimes difficult; and then it helps a little if one can nibble the slate pencil, isn't that so, General?"

"Yes, that's true," acknowledged Peter.

Now Heidi's interest was thoroughly aroused. She asked Peter many questions about school and everything to be seen and heard there. Since conversation with Peter was inclined to be a slow business he had ample opportunity to get thoroughly dry. He always had great difficulty in putting his thoughts into words and on the subject of school this was particularly hard. By the time he had managed to think of the answer to one question Heidi had already thought of two or three more to ask and they were all of a kind which required much answering. The grandfather kept silent during this dialogue but an occasional twitch of amusement at the corners of his mouth showed that he was listening.

"Well, General, now you have been under fire and must be in need of some refreshment!" As he spoke, the old man rose and got the supper from the cupboard and Heidi brought the chairs up to the table.

Peter's round eyes opened wider when he saw what a large piece of delicious meat the grandfather put on his plate. He had not enjoyed himself so much for a long time. As they finished the meal it began to grow dark and Peter prepared to go home. He had already bid them good night, but turned again at the door and said: "I'll come back again on Sunday, a week to-day, but the grandmother said she would like you to come to see her sometime."

This new idea of going to visit somebody appealed to Heidi at once and on the following morning her first words were, "Grandfather, I must go down and see the grandmother to-day. She will be expecting me."

"The snow is too deep," replied the grandfather to put her off. But Heidi was determined to go since she had got the grandmother's message. Not a day passed without her pleading, "Grandfather, I must go now! The grandmother is waiting for me!"

On the fourth day a hard frost had set in and the ground crackled at every step. But the bright sun peeped in at the window and fell on Heidi where she sat on her high chair at the table. Soon she had begun her customary little speech, "To-day I must go to the grandmother or she will be tired of waiting for me."

The grandfather rose and going up to the hayloft brought down the thick sack which was Heidi's bed-cover. "Come, then!" he said. Joyously the child skipped out into the glittering snow world. The old fir trees were silent now and on every branch the snow lay thickly.

The grandfather went into the shed and brought out a large sleigh. There was a pole fixed at the side and from the low seat the sleigh could be guided by the feet pressing against the ground and with the help of the pole.

The grandfather took his seat on the sleigh and placed the child on his knee, wrapping her carefully in the sack to keep her warm. His left arm held her secure and this was necessary for the long drive ahead. Then he grasped the pole with his right hand and gave a push with his feet. The sleigh shot down the Alm with such rapidity that Heidi felt she was flying through the air like a bird. She shouted aloud with joy.

By and by the sleigh stopped with a jerk just outside Goat Peter's cottage. The grandfather lifted the child and unwrapped her, saying, "Now in you go and when

it starts to get dark come straight home!" Then he
turned and pulled the sleigh back up the mountain.

Heidi opened the cottage door and found herself in
a small, rather dark room. She could see a fireplace
and a shelf with some dishes so she concluded that this
was the kitchen. Then she saw a door and she found
that it led into another, narrower room. This cottage
was quite different from her grandfather's and everything looked very poor and shabby. When Heidi entered
the room she saw a table, and at the table a woman was
sitting patching a jacket which Heidi recognised at
once as Peter's. In the corner, an old bent woman sat
spinning. Heidi went straight to her. "Good day,
Grandmother!" she said. "Here I am to see you. Did
you think I was long in coming?"

The old woman lifted her head and groped for the
hand which Heidi held out to her. When she had found
it she held it for a while, thoughtfully. Then she said,
"Are you the child who stays with the Alm-Uncle? Are
you Heidi?"

"Yes," said Heidi. "I have just come down in the
sleigh with Grandfather."

"How can it be? Your hands are quite warm. Brigitta,
did the Alm-Uncle himself come with the child?"

Peter's mother, Brigitta, who had been mending at
the table got up and looked curiously at the little girl.
"I don't know, Mother," she said. "I suppose the child
knows if the Alm-Uncle came himself."

Heidi looked at the woman and said firmly, "I know
very well who wrapped me in the cover and brought me
down in the sleigh. It was Grandfather."

"Then there must be something in what Peter said
about the Alm-Uncle although we didn't believe him
at the time," said the grandmother. "Who could believe
it possible! I didn't think the child would stay up there

more than three weeks. How does she look, Brigitta?"

By this time Brigitta had carefully inspected Heidi from every angle so she was able to report: "She is as finely built as Adelheid was, but she has the dark eyes and curly hair of Tobias and the old man. I think she resembles both her parents."

During this time, Heidi's attention had not been idle. She had looked round carefully at everything in the room. Suddenly she said, "Look, Grandmother! One of your shutters is loose. The grandfather would put a nail in and then the shutter would be all right. It will break the window-pane soon. See how it shakes!"

"Ah, my child," said the grandmother, "I can't see but I can hear, and much more than the shutter banging. Everything in this house creaks and rattles as soon as the wind blows. It comes in from all sides. Everything seems to be loose. During the night, when the others are asleep, I often fear that the house is going to fall to pieces and kill us all. Alas, there is no one here to repair things. Peter doesn't know how to."

"But can't you see the shutter banging, Grandmother? Look! There it is, just over there!" said Heidi, pointing towards the shutter.

"Alas, child, I can see nothing, nothing!" lamented the grandmother.

"But if I go outside and open the shutter properly so that it is lighter, won't you see then, Grandmother?"

"No, not even then. Nobody can ever make it light for me."

"But if you go outside into the white snow then surely it will be light. Come with me, Grandmother, and I will show you." Heidi, beginning to feel very distressed, took the old woman's hand and tried to lead her.

"Just let me sit, child. It will always be dark for me."

"But surely in summer it will be different, Grandmother," comforted Heidi, becoming more and more anxious to help. "Surely then it will be light for you! When the sun shines on the mountains and on the flowers and turns them all to crimson."

"Ah, child, I shall never again see the flaming mountains nor the little golden flowers up there. It will never again be light for me on this earth, never!"

Suddenly, Heidi began to cry. Full of compassion she sobbed, "Who then can help you? Is there no one?"

The grandmother tried to comfort the child. The old woman was touched to hear her sob so bitterly. Heidi rarely cried, but when she did her grief was not easily overcome. At last the grandmother said, "Come, my dear Heidi, come and I will explain something to you. You see, when one can't see one likes to hear a kind word and I like to hear you talking. Come, sit here close to me and tell me what you have been doing up there and all about the grandfather. I knew him very well years ago. But for many years now I have only heard of him from Peter, and Peter doesn't talk much."

Suddenly, Heidi had a new idea. Quickly she wiped away her tears and said comfortingly, "You wait, Grandmother, and I shall tell Grandfather everything. He will make it light for you again and will repair the cottage for you. He can do everything."

The grandmother was silent now and Heidi began to give a lively account of her life, of summer days on the pasture and her present life in winter with the grandfather. She described the things he could make from wood—benches and chairs and beautiful mangers where the hay was put for Little Swan and Little Bear, and a big new tub for bathing in summer, a new milk bowl and a spoon. Heidi was quite carried away describing all the beautiful things which could be made from pieces of wood. The grandmother listened intently and every now and then she would say, "Do you hear, Brigitta? Do you hear what she says about the Alm-Uncle?"

Suddenly the story was interrupted by a loud clatter at the door and in tramped Peter. He stopped abruptly and gaped when he saw Heidi, but managed a friendly grin as she greeted him, "Good evening, Peter!"

"Is the boy back from school already?" asked the grandmother in surprise. "An afternoon has not passed so quickly for me for a long time! Good evening, Peter. How did you get on with your reading to-day?"

"Just as usual," answered Peter.

"Well, well," sighed the grandmother gently. "I thought there might perhaps be a change by this time, especially as you are going to be twelve years old in February."

"What do you mean by change, Grandmother?" Heidi asked with interest.

"I hoped he would be able to learn to read," explained the grandmother. "Up there on the shelf is an old hymn book with beautiful hymns in it. I have not heard them for a very long time and I can't remember them now. So I had hoped if Peter could learn to read he would be able to read the hymns to me. But he can't learn the letters. It is too difficult for him."

"I think I had better light the lamp. It is getting quite dark," said Peter's mother, who was still busy patching his jacket. "This afternoon has flown by without my noticing."

Heidi jumped up from her chair, stretched out her hand quickly to the grandmother and said, "Good-bye, Grandmother. I have to go home when it gets dark." She said good night to Peter and his mother and went towards the door. But the grandmother called anxiously, "Wait, wait, Heidi! You mustn't go alone. Peter will go with you. Do you hear? Take care of the child, Peter, and see that she doesn't fall down. And don't loiter on the way in case she catches cold, do you hear? Has she got a warm scarf?"

"I haven't got a scarf," replied Heidi, " but I shall not be cold."

With these words she was outside the house and away so quickly that Peter could hardly keep pace. "Run after her, Brigitta!" the grandmother called. "The child will be frozen to death on such a night. Take my scarf! Run quickly!"

Brigitta obeyed. The children had only gone a little way up the mountain when they saw the grandfather coming down and soon he stood beside them.

"Good, Heidi! You have kept your word," he praised her. Then wrapping her snugly in the cover he picked her up and turned back up the mountain.

Brigitta saw the old man lift the child, well wrapped up, into his arms. She returned with Peter to the cottage and told the grandmother with amusement what she had seen.

The grandmother was both astonished and glad. "God be thanked that he is good to the child! If only he would allow her to come again! She is a great comfort and what a kind heart she has!" Until the grandmother went to bed she kept repeating, "If only she could come again! Then I might have something to look forward to in this world!"

All the way, Heidi chatted to the grandfather although he could not make out a word of the muffled voice coming from inside the sack. So he said, "Wait until we get home, then you can tell me all about it."

As soon as they entered the hut and Heidi was released from her wrapping she said, "Grandfather, to-morrow we must take the hammer and plenty of long nails to fix the grandmother's shutters and all the loose boards because her house rattles and shakes all over!"

"Must we, indeed! And who told you so?" inquired the grandfather.

"Nobody told me but I know myself," replied Heidi, "for everything is loose and if the grandmother cannot sleep she is afraid that any minute the house will fall down on their heads. And for her everything is dark and she thinks that nobody can ever make it light for her again; but you can do it, Grandfather, I am sure. Think how sad it is for her always having to sit in the dark, and being frightened; and only you can help her. To-morrow we will go and help her, won't we, Grandfather?"

Heidi clung tightly to the grandfather and looked up at him with eagerness and confidence. For a little while the old man looked down at the child, then he said, " Yes, Heidi, we will go and see about the repairs. We can do that to-morrow."

The child started to skip round the room, chanting joyfully, " To-morrow we'll go! To-morrow we'll go!"

The grandfather kept his promise and on the following afternoon they took the same sleigh drive as they had done the previous day. Once again the old man set the child down before the door of Goat Peter's cottage and said, " Go in now and come away again whenever it gets dark!"

Scarcely had Heidi opened the door and skipped into the room when the grandmother called from her corner, "It is Heidi! Here comes the child!" In her eagerness, she let the thread drop from her fingers and the wheel stood still as both her arms stretched out towards the child. Heidi ran to her at once, and drawing the little chair close to her she sat down at her side. Once again there was so much she had to tell the grandmother and

so many questions she had to ask. But suddenly such
heavy blows sounded against the wall that the grandmother started violently and nearly upset the spinning
wheel. "Mercy on us!" she exclaimed, trembling.
"What is that? The house must be falling about us!"
Heidi grasped her arm firmly and comforted her, "No,
no, Grandmother! Don't be afraid! It is only Grandfather hammering. He will fix everything so that you
don't need to be afraid any more."

"Is it possible? Then the Lord has not forgotten us!"
the grandmother exclaimed. "Did you hear that,
Brigitta? If it is the Alm-Uncle, go and tell him to come
in so that I can thank him!"

Brigitta went outside. The Alm-Uncle was busy nail-
ing some strong planks to the wall, knocking in the
nails with great vigour. Brigitta approached and said,
"Good evening, Uncle! Mother and I want to thank
you for your kindness and she would like to tell you
herself how grateful she is."

"That will do," interrupted the old man. "I know
what you think of the Alm-Uncle. Go back inside. I can
find out for myself what is needed here."

Brigitta obeyed at once for the Uncle expressed himself in a way which brooked no opposition.

He knocked and hammered his way all round the
house and then climbed the narrow little stair up to
the roof, and hammered away there until he had used his
last nail. By the time he had finished, darkness had fallen
and he had no sooner come down and got out the sleigh
from behind the shed than Heidi appeared. As on the
previous day, the grandfather wrapped her up and took
her in his arms, and, dragging the sleigh behind, made his
way back up the mountain.

And so the winter passed. After many lonely years
a great happiness had entered the joyless life of the old

blind grandmother, and her days were no longer dreary and dark for now she had something to look forward to. From early morning she listened for Heidi's familiar tripping steps. The child became very attached to the old grandmother. As soon as she understood that nobody, not even the grandfather, could help the old woman she was very sad; but the grandmother told her again and again that she felt the darkness much less when Heidi was with her. So every fine winter's day Heidi came down on the sleigh. Without any fuss, the grandfather always packed in his tools and he spent many afternoons repairing the cottage. All his good work soon had its effect and the cottage no longer rattled and groaned when the wind blew around it. The grandmother said she had not slept so well for many a year and that she would never forget what the Alm-Uncle had done for her.

CHAPTER 5

Two Visitors to the Alm-Hut

~~~~~~~~~~

QUICKLY THE winter passed, and more quickly still the happy days of summer; and now another winter was drawing to its close. Heidi was happy as a bird and each day she looked forward eagerly to the coming of spring when the warm south wind would sweep through the fir trees and across the valley, melting the last patch of snow on the lower slopes. Long days on the pasture would return and this seemed to Heidi the greatest joy of all. She was eight years old now and had learnt a great deal during the time she had lived with the Alm-Uncle. She knew how to manage the goats, and Little Swan and Little Bear would follow her about, bleating at the very sound of her voice.

Twice during this winter Peter had come from the school in Dorfli with a message from the teacher telling the Alm-Uncle that the child he had staying with him should go to school since she was over the age and should, indeed, have attended the previous winter. On both occasions, the Alm-Uncle had replied that he had no intention of sending the child to school.

One sunny morning in March, as Heidi ran out of the house, she was startled to come face to face with an old gentleman dressed in black. He stood regarding her gravely for a time and then, thinking that his unexpected appearance had frightened her, he said kindly, " It is all right. You need not be afraid of me. You are Heidi, are you not? Where is your grandfather?"

38

"He is sitting at the table, making wooden spoons," replied Heidi and at once led him inside.

It was the old pastor from Dörfli who had known the uncle well in the old days. He walked towards the old man who was bent over his work, and addressed him.

"Good morning, neighbour!"

Astonished, the grandfather looked up, then rose, saying, "Good morning, pastor!" Offering his seat to the visitor, he added, "Pray sit down."

The pastor seated himself. "I have not seen you for a long time, neighbour," he said.

"Nor I you!"

"I have come to-day to discuss something with you," continued the pastor. "I think perhaps you know what it is I want to talk to you about, and that I am anxious to hear what you intend to do about a certain matter."

There was a silence. The pastor glanced quickly towards the child, who stood by the door and watched the newcomer with interest.

"Heidi, go and see how the goats are getting along!" said the grandfather. "You may take them a little salt, and stay with them until I come!"

Heidi disappeared at once.

"The child should have gone to school a year ago," said the pastor now. "The schoolmaster reminded you more than once but you ignored him. What is it you intend should become of the child, neighbour?"

"I intend that she should *not* go to school!"

The pastor looked with surprise at the old man who sat on his bench with his arms folded determinedly.

"But how is the child going to grow up?" asked the pastor reasonably.

"She will grow up with the goats and birds. That way she will learn nothing evil."

"But the child is neither a goat nor a bird but a

human being," pleaded the pastor. "Though she learns nothing evil from her companions, they cannot teach her her A B C! Learn she must, and the time has come to begin. I came to speak a word to you in time, neighbour, so that you may think it over at your leisure and make arrangements during the summer. The child must not be allowed to run about another winter without taking lessons. Next winter she must attend school regularly!"

"No, she will not go, pastor!" muttered the old man with unwavering determination.

"Do you really think there is no way of making you see reason if you insist so stubbornly on this decision?" asked the pastor, beginning to lose patience. "You have lived in the world and have seen and learnt a lot. I should have thought you would have had more sense, neighbour."

"You think so?" asked the old man, and the tremor in his voice betrayed that he was no longer calm. "And do you really think that next winter I shall send a delicate child on a two hours' walk down the mountain on ice-cold mornings in storm and snow, and allow her to return at night when there may be a wind raging fit to blow a man over, let alone a child? Perhaps the pastor still remembers the child's mother, Adelheid. She was a sleep-walker and had a delicate constitution. Might not the health of this child, who is also finely built, be endangered by so much exertion? I wonder who can force me to send her? I shall take it to the highest law court in the country and then we shall see who can force me!"

"You are quite right, neighbour," agreed the pastor, amicably. "It would not be possible to send the child from here. But I see the child is dear to you. For her sake, do what you ought to have done long ago. Come down into Dorfli and live amongst us! What a life you live here, alone and embittered towards God and men. If anything should happen to you up here in the mountains who would come to your assistance? I cannot understand how you are not frozen to death in this hut of yours in the winter-time. How does this delicate child stand up to it?"

"I see to it that she is not cold, and that she has a good warm bed, I should like the pastor to know. And another thing : I get all the wood I need. If the pastor cares to look into my wood-shed he will soon see! There is plenty there! The fire is never out in my hut all through the winter. As for living down in the valley, it is out of the question. The people down there despise me and I them. For all our sakes, it is better we stay apart."

"No, no, you are quite wrong!" the pastor said warmly. "The people down below don't dislike you half as much as you think. Take my advice, neighbour! Make your peace with God, ask His forgiveness and then come and see how people will change towards you and how happy you will be!"

The pastor rose. He held out his hand to the old man and repeated with kindly emphasis, "I am counting on it, neighbour! Next winter you'll come back to live with us in the valley and we'll be good neighbours again, as we used to be. I would be disappointed to think that you were coming back only because of the school business. Promise me that you will live amongst us again, reconciled to God and man!"

The Alm-Uncle shook hands with the pastor but insisted firmly, "I know you mean well, but as to what you expect me to do—no! Once and for all I tell you I will not send the child, nor will I come down to live in the valley."

" Then God help you ! " sighed the pastor and sadly made his way down the mountain.

As a result of the interview, the Alm-Uncle was in a very black mood, and when Heidi asked in the afternoon, "Shall we go down to the grandmother's now?" he replied harshly, "Not to-day!" He was silent the whole day and the following morning, when Heidi asked again, "Shall we go to-day to see the grandmother?" he turned away abruptly, mumbling, "Perhaps."

But before the dinner dishes had been cleared away another visitor had arrived. It was cousin Dete, dressed in a beautiful gown which swept the floor and wearing on her head a very fine hat with feathers. The Alm-Uncle examined her from head to foot in amazement. But Dete was all prepared to make friendly conversation and at once adopted a flattering tone.

"How well the child looks! I hardly recognised her! I can see that she has not had a bad time with the Alm-Uncle, far from it! I have often thought of taking the child back for I can imagine that she is in your way. Day and night I have thought about what to do with her and that's why I am here to-day. I have just heard of something that would be a piece of luck for Heidi. I have fixed everything. It is really a wonderful chance. The people I am in service with have some very wealthy relations. They live in the most beautiful house in Frankfurt and they have an only daughter who is an invalid and has to be wheeled in a chair. She is very much alone and has her lessons with a private teacher, which, of course, is very boring for her. Now she would like a playmate so her people have asked my mistress to help them find a companion. The lady house-keeper thinks that a simple, unspoilt child, one different from the children now-a-days, would be most suitable. Naturally I thought of Heidi and went at once to the lady and told her all about our child's character. She agreed immediately to take her. No one can foresee what good fortune will be in store for Heidi. If the people become fond of her and if something should happen to their own little daughter—and who knows when she is so weak—then in all likelihood they would not want to be without a child—then it would be the most unheard-of luck——"

"Do you think you have just about finished?" interrupted the Alm-Uncle who had held his peace up till now.

"Ugh!" exclaimed Dete, tossing her head. "You behave as though I were telling you something of no consequence. Anybody in Prattigau would thank God if I were to bring such news!"

"You may take your news where you like. I want to hear no more of it," replied the Uncle dryly.

This threw Dete immediately into a passion. "Well!" she stormed, "if that is all you have to say, Uncle, I will speak my mind, too. The child is eight years old now, but she knows nothing. You neither want her to attend school nor to go to church. Oh, I have heard all about it in Dorfli. She is my sister's child and I am responsible for what happens to her. When such a good chance comes her way only who cared nothing for her welfare would oppose it. But I tell you, I won't give in and people are on my side. There is not a single person who would not take my part—and they are all against you. And if you are thinking of taking it to law, think well, Uncle! There are things could be brought up against you which you wouldn't like to hear."

"Hold your tongue!" thundered the uncle, his eyes ablaze with anger. "Very well, then. Take the child away and ruin her! And never let me set eyes on you again, with that ridiculous hat on your head and such words on your tongue!" Then the uncle turned from her abruptly and strode from the hut.

"You have made Grandfather angry," said Heidi, fixing dark, smouldering eyes on her aunt.

"Oh, he'll soon get over it," replied Dete impatiently. "Come along now! Where are your clothes?"

"I won't go!" said Heidi defiantly.

"What did you say?" asked the aunt, about to fly into a temper. Then she softened her tone a little and continued more persuasively, "Come, come! You don't know any better. You have no idea how well off you will be." Then, going to the wardrobe, she took out Heidi's things and parcelled them together. "Come now! Here is your hat! What a sight it is! But never mind! It will do for to-day. Put it on, quickly."

"I am going to stay here," repeated Heidi.

"Don't be so silly. You are as obstinate as a goat. I suppose that is what you have learnt from them. But you've got to understand, the grandfather is cross and doesn't want to see us again, you heard him say so. He wants you to go with me, so now you mustn't make him more angry. You have no idea how nice it is in Frankfurt. But, of course, if you don't like it you can always come back here. By that time the grandfather will have recovered himself."

"Can I come straight home again if I want to?" asked Heidi.

"Come along now and don't be silly! I said you can go home when you like. To-day we are only going as far as Maienfeld but to-morrow we will travel by train, and the train can carry you home again as fast as the wind."

Aunt Dete took the bundle of clothes under one arm, grasped Heidi firmly by the other hand, and together they started to climb down the hill.

Peter had just come round the side of the cottage, carrying a huge bundle of thick hazel twigs, when the two figures approached. He stopped to stare at them as they passed by; then he called out after them, "Where are you going?"

"I have to go at once to Frankfurt with Aunt," answered Heidi, "but I am going to say good-bye to the grandmother first. She will be waiting for me."

"No, no," interrupted the aunt quickly. "It is much too late. You can see her next time you come back. Come along, now!" And she pulled the child along, afraid that she might again take it into her head to stay.

Peter dashed into the cottage and dropped his bundle of sticks so noisily that the grandmother started up from her spinning, exclaiming fretfully, "What is it now? What is it?" And Peter's mother, who had been sitting by the table, said in her patient way, "What is it, Peter? What is the matter?"

"She is taking Heidi away!" gasped Peter.

"Who?" asked the grandmother in distress. "Taking her where, Peter?" But she soon guessed what had taken place, for her daughter had told her not long ago that she had seen Dete going up to the Alm-Uncle's. The old woman unfastened the window with trembling fingers and called out imploringly, "Dete, Dete, don't take the child away from us! Don't take Heidi away!"

Dete and Heidi heard the voice. Dete had evidently made out the grandmother's words for she grasped the child's hand still more firmly and ran as fast as she could.

Heidi, struggling to get her hand free, cried, "The grandmother is calling! I want to go to her!"

But that was exactly what the aunt did not want. She tried to soothe the child. "Come quickly now or it will be too late and we will not be able to continue our journey to-morrow. You will soon see how much you will like Frankfurt. Perhaps you will never want to come back again. But if you do it will be quite simple.

You could even take something home for the grandmother—something she would like."

This appealed to Heidi and she stopped trying to
resist and started to run, too.

After a little while she asked, "What could I get for
Grandmother?"

"Something nice," said the aunt. "Perhaps some nice
soft rolls. She would enjoy that. It would be such a
change from the dark bread."

"Oh, yes! She always gives it to Peter and says ' It
is too hard for me.' I have heard her myself," admitted
Heidi. "Let us hurry, then, Aunt Dete! We may reach
Frankfurt to-day and I shall soon be back with the rolls."
And Heidi started to run so fast that the aunt with her
bundle could hardly keep pace with her. But she was glad
to be having no more difficulty with the child for now
they had almost reached the first houses in Dorfli and a
lot of talk and questions might have made Heidi change
her mind again. So Dete strode straight ahead holding
Heidi's hand tightly so that every one would see that she
had to hurry along because of the child. To every
question she merely answered, "I can't stop now. We
have a long way to go."

Questions and exclamations came from all sides
and Dete was glad that she didn't have to stop and that
Heidi didn't say a word but hurried on eagerly.

From that day on the Alm-Uncle looked even more
fierce and terrifying when he came down to Dorfli. He
spoke to no one and looked most threatening with his
cheese-basket on his back and his mountain stick in his
hand. Everybody was of the same opinion; that it was
a great blessing that the child had been taken away.
Only the blind grandmother took the old man's part.
When people came to the house to give her some spinning
to do, she would tell them again and again how kind

C

and good he had been to the child and what he had done for herself and her daughter; how he had spent many afternoons repairing the cottage which, without his help, would undoubtedly have collapsed upon them. This story soon got about in Dorfli, but most people thought the grandmother was too old to understand and too blind and hard of hearing to know exactly what went on around her.

It was as well it had been repaired, for the Alm-Uncle never came to Goat Peter's cottage now and the grandmother's days were once more passed in sighing and fretting. "Alas, all the joy and happiness has gone with the child!" she would say, "and the days are long and dreary! If only I might see Heidi again before I die!"

CHAPTER 6

A New Start for Heidi

━━━━━━━

N THE HOUSE in Frankfurt, the little daughter of Herr Sesemann sat in the comfortable invalid chair in which all her life was spent and in which she had to be wheeled from room to room. Now she was in the room which they called the study, and where she had her lessons.

Clara's little face was pale and thin and her soft, gentle blue eyes were fixed at this moment on the door. To-day, time seemed to pass very slowly for her, for she was saying rather impatiently, "But isn't it time yet, Fraulein Rottenmeier?"

The lady thus addressed sat very upright at a small work-table and nodded. Principally because of her rather odd and very severe style of dress, Fraulein Rottenmeier presented an awe-inspiring appearance. Over her shoulders she wore a cape with a stiff collar and on her head a very elaborate cap. Since the death of Frau Sesemann, several years ago, Fraulein Rottenmeier had acted as housekeeper and manager of the domestic staff. Herr Sesemann very often went off on business trips, leaving Fraulein Rottenmeier in sole charge of the house, stipulating only that no decisions should be taken without first consulting his little daughter and that nothing should be done against her wish.

Just as Clara was asking the same question a second time, Dete and Heidi arrived at the door.

Dete rang the bell and the butler came down the stairs, the big round buttons of his livery in keeping with his round eyes which stared blankly at the two strangers.

"I wonder if it is too late to see Fraulein Rottenmeier?" Dete asked.

Sebastian stared frostily for a moment, then pressed a bell and disappeared without a word. Next a maid appeared. A spotless white cap was perched on top of her head. Regarding the visitors haughtily from the top of the stairs, "What is it?" she asked.

Dete repeated her request. Tinette disappeared, but very soon came back and called from above, "Come this way! You are expected."

Dete and Heidi went upstairs and followed Tinette into the study. At the door Dete stopped politely, still holding Heidi's hand firmly for there was no knowing what the child might do in strange surroundings.

Fraulein Rottenmeier rose slowly and came forward to examine the new playmate for the daughter of the house. She did not appear to be very pleased with what she saw. Heidi wore her simple little cotton dress and on her head, her old, crushed, straw hat. She gazed innocently from underneath it, staring with unconcealed surprise at the lady's towering headgear.

"What is your name?" asked Fraulein Rottenmeier, after a lengthy inspection of the child, who had returned her gaze steadily.

"Heidi," the child answered distinctly.

"What? That is not a Christian name! You were surely not baptised so! What name were you given when you were christened?"

"I can't remember now," replied Heidi.

"What a foolish answer!" exclaimed the lady, shaking her head disapprovingly. "Dete, is the child stupid or impertinent?"

"I am so sorry! Would you kindly allow me to speak for the child? She is not accustomed to strangers," said

Dete hastily, secretly nudging Heidi for having given such an unsuitable answer. "She certainly is not stupid, nor impertinent. It is just that she always says exactly what she is thinking. This is the first time she has ever been in an upper-class house and she knows nothing about good manners. She is docile and willing to learn if madam will have the patience. She was christened Adelheid for her mother, my late sister."

"Well, at least that's a name one can pronounce," remarked Fraulein Rottenmeier. "But Dete, I must say that for her age the child looks to me a little strange. I told you that a companion for Fraulein Clara had to be of her age to be able to share her lessons and everything. Fraulein Clara is twelve now. What is the age of the child?"

"With your permission," began Dete elaborately, "I am not quite sure myself but I think she is a little younger, but not much. She will be ten, or perhaps a little more."

"I am eight now, the grandfather said," declared Heidi. The aunt gave her another push but Heidi had no idea of the reason for this and was not in the least embarrassed.

"What! Only eight years old!" cried Fraulein Rottenmeier indignantly. "Four years younger! What use is that? And what have you learnt? Which books did you use for your lessons?"

"None," replied Heidi.

"What? How did you learn to read?"

"I never learnt. Neither did Peter," said Heidi.

"Mercy! You cannot read! Is that true that you cannot read?" demanded Fraulein Rottenmeier, deeply shocked. "What did you learn, then?"

"Nothing," said Heidi.

"Dete!" cried Fraulein Rottenmeier when she had

recovered from this shock. "This is not the agreement at all! How dare you bring this child to me!"

But Dete was not easily frightened and replied boldly, "With madam's permission, the child is just what I understood madam wanted. Madam told me she wanted a companion unlike ordinary children. Therefore I chose this one because the older ones are not so unspoilt. But now I am afraid I must go. My mistress will be expecting me. If I may, I shall come again soon to see how the child is getting on."

With a curtsy, Dete left the room and quickly ran downstairs. For a moment Fraulein Rottenmeier was too surprised to speak, then she ran after Dete. There were many things which must be discussed if the child were to stay and the aunt seemed determined that she should.

Heidi still stood by the door. So far Clara had watched silently; now she beckoned to Heidi to come nearer.

Heidi went up to her.

"Would you rather be called Heidi or Adelheid?" asked Clara.

"I am always called Heidi," Heidi replied.

"Then I shall always call you that, too," said Clara. "I like the name although never before have I seen a little girl like you. Has your hair always been short and curly like that?"

"Yes, I think so," replied Heidi.

"Did you come to Frankfurt yesterday?" Clara continued to ask.

"No, to-day. But to-morrow I am going home again with some white rolls for the grandmother."

"How strange you are!" Clara burst out. "You have been brought here to stay with me and share my lessons with me. What fun it will be now because you can't read at all. At least it will be a change. It is usually very dull and the mornings are so long! You see, every morning at ten my tutor comes and the lessons go on till two. That is far too long! Sometimes the tutor holds his book close to his face as if he had suddenly become shortsighted but I know quite well it is only because he is yawning; and Fraulein Rottenmeier takes out her handkerchief and holds it to her face as if she were affected by what we are reading, but she too only wants to yawn. But I don't dare, because if I only did it once Fraulein Rottenmeier would fetch the cod liver oil and say I was getting weak again, and the worst thing of all is to take cod liver oil. But it will be much more fun now. I can listen to you learning to read."

Heidi shook her head doubtfully at the mention of her learning to read.

"Of course, Heidi, you have to learn to read. Everybody has to learn to read and my tutor is very kind. He is never cross and he will explain everything to you."

Just then Fraulein Rottenmeier came back into the room. She had not succeeded in calling Dete back and was apparently very annoyed about it. Sebastian had opened the folding doors of the study and quietly wheeled Clara into the other room. While he adjusted the chair Heidi placed herself before him and stared steadily up at him.

"Well, what is it you are looking at?" he grumbled.

When Fraulein Rottenmeier returned she was just in time to hear Heidi say, "You look like Peter."

She raised her hands in horror. "Really!" she murmured. "She treats the butler as an equal! The child knows absolutely nothing!"

Sebastian helped Clara to her seat at the table and Fraulein Rottenmeier seated herself beside her, motioning Heidi to sit opposite. Beside Heidi's plate lay a lovely

white roll. She glanced at it happily. The resemblance
Heidi had discovered in Sebastian seemed to have given
her confidence in him for she sat as quiet as a mouse until
he came to her side to serve the fish, then she pointed to
the roll and asked, "May I have it?"

Sebastian nodded, glancing sideways at Fraulein
Rottenmeier to see what effect the question had had on
her.

Immediately Heidi took the roll and put it into her
pocket. Sebastian hid a smile. Motionless and silent,
he stood at her side, waiting for her to take her helping of
fish. For a few seconds Heidi looked at him wonderingly,
then she asked, "May I have a little of that, too?" Sebastian
nodded again. "Then give me some, please," she said,
looking calmly at her plate. At this breach of etiquette
Sebastian was almost in danger of losing control of
his features and the arm which held the dish was beginning to shake.

"You can leave the dish on the table and come back
afterwards," ordered Fraulein Rottenmeier, looking very
severe, and Sebastian disappeared at once.

"Adelheid, I see I shall have to teach you the first
simple rules of good behaviour," said the lady with a deep
sigh. "First of all I will show you how to behave at
table."

She instructed Heidi thoroughly and clearly on what
she had to do. "Then," she went on to explain, "I must
impress upon you particularly that you are not to speak
to Sebastian at table unless the question or remark is
absolutely necessary, and even then you must not address
him as a friend. Do you understand? And so with
Tinette. You will address *me* as you hear others do.
Clara will decide for herself what you are to call her."

"Clara, of course!" Clara interrupted.

Then followed a long list of rules about getting up

and going to bed, about entering and leaving a room, about being tidy and shutting doors. All of a sudden Heidi's eyes closed, for she had been up since five o'clock that morning and had had a long journey. She leaned back in her chair, fast asleep. When Fraulein Rottenmeier had finished her lecture at last, she said, "Now, remember everything I have said, Adelheid! Have you understood it all?"

"Heidi has been asleep for ever so long," Clara said with amusement. She had not had such an entertaining dinner for a long time!

"It is really shocking how much trouble this child is causing," exclaimed Fraulein Rottenmeier angrily and rang the bell so violently that both Sebastian and Tinette came rushing in. But in spite of all the noise Heidi slept on and it was only with great difficulty that they succeeded in awakening her so that she could be shown to her bedroom which was at the end of a long passage, beyond those of Clara and Fraulein Rottenmeier.

CHAPTER 7

An Eventful Day

∼∼∼∼∼∼∼∼∼

HEIDI AWOKE in the morning and looked around in bewilderment. She blinked and rubbed her eyes but it did not help her to remember where she was. She was lying in a high white bed in a big room and daylight streamed in between long white curtains. There were two arm-chairs covered in a floral material. A sofa stood against the wall with a round table in front of it and in the corner there was a wash-stand.

Suddenly she remembered that she was in Frankfurt and the events of the previous day came back to her quite clearly. She jumped out of bed and dressed; then went from one window to the other to try to get a glimpse of the sky and the countryside outside. Behind the big curtains she felt like a bird in a cage. As she could not manage to pull them aside she crept underneath to get to the window. It was so high that she could only just see over the sill. However, the view was not one of pleasant green fields but only of walls and windows. Presently there came a knock at the door and Tinette popped her head round, saying in a bored voice, "Break-fast is ready!"

Heidi failed to understand that this was an invitation, for the sour expression on Tinette's face had suggested rather a warning to stay away. So it seemed to Heidi, at any rate, and she acted accordingly. She took the little stool from under the table, put it in a corner, sat down and waited quietly to see what would happen next. After some time Fraulein Rottenmeier bustled

55

along with a great deal of noise. Once again she seemed to be thoroughly annoyed and shouted at Heidi, "What is the matter with you, Adelheid? Don't you know what breakfast is? Come along!"

This Heidi understood and followed at once. Clara had been seated in the dining-room for some time and she greeted Heidi in a friendly way. Her face wore a much happier expression than usual for she was looking forward to all kinds of unexpected events that day. Breakfast passed without incident. Heidi ate her rolls very nicely and when they had finished Clara was wheeled back to the study. Fraulein Rottenmeier told Heidi to follow and remain with Clara until the tutor arrived to begin lessons. As soon as the children were alone together Heidi asked, "How can I see right down to the ground?"

"You just open the window and look out!" replied Clara, amused.

"But the windows won't open," replied Heidi sadly.

"Oh, yes," Clara assured her, "but you can't do it alone. Neither can I. But if you see Sebastian he will open them for you."

Heidi sighed with relief, for the house had begun to make her feel as though she were a prisoner. Then Clara began to ask Heidi about her home and Heidi was delighted to tell her all about the Alm and the goats and the pasture and everything that was dear to her.

In the meantime the tutor had arrived, but Fraulein Rottenmeier did not show him into the study as usual. She wanted to talk to him first and led him to the dining-room. There, in great agitation, she began to describe to him the awkward situation which had arisen and told him how, some time ago, she had persuaded Herr Sesemann to get a companion for Clara. She recounted how dreadfully she had been deceived and told the tutor how, in view of Heidi's complete ignorance, he would have to begin at the very beginning with the A B C, and how she herself had had to give the child instruction on the simplest rules of behaviour. There was only one way out of the situation, in Fraulein Rottenmeier's opinion, and that was for the tutor to insist that it was impossible to teach two children so far apart in age without retarding Clara's progress. That would be a very good reason for Herr Sesemann's sending the child back home. Herr Sesemann knew the child had arrived and without his consent Fraulein Rottenmeier could not send her away again.

However, the tutor was cautious and unwilling to commit himself. With many words of comfort he assured Fraulein Rottenmeier that though the child were backward in some things she might be quite advanced in other respects and that regular lessons might very well restore the balance. When Fraulein Rottenmeier at last realised that she would get very little support from the tutor she opened the door to the study and allowed him to go through to the children.

Before many minutes had passed, a dreadful noise came from the study. Then there was a loud cry from Sebastian. Fraulein Rottenmeier rushed in to find the whole room in complete disorder; books, copybooks, ink-stand; and across the table, on to the floor and across the carpet there flowed a stream of ink. Heidi was nowhere to be seen.

"What is all this?" cried Fraulein Rottenmeier. "Carpet, books, work basket, everything covered with ink! I never saw such a mess! I have no doubt that wretched child is to blame!"

The tutor looked very distressed but Clara was following events with obvious amusement.

"Yes, Heidi did it, but not on purpose. She mustn't be punished. It was just that she was in such a hurry to get away that she tugged the table-cloth and then everything fell on the floor. She wanted to see the carriages passing; that's why she rushed out. Perhaps she has never seen one before!"

"What did I tell you? The creature doesn't know the first thing! She has no idea what a lesson is—that she must sit still and listen. But where is the little trouble-maker? Surely she hasn't run away! Whatever will Herr Sesemann say?"

Fraulein Rottenmeier ran downstairs. There stood Heidi in the open doorway looking out into the street in complete bewilderment.

"What is the matter? What are you thinking of to run away like that?" Fraulein Rottenmeier shouted at the child.

"I thought I heard the fir trees rustling but I can't find them and I don't hear them any more," said Heidi disconsolately, turning her head in the direction of the disappearing carriages. The rumbling of their wheels had seemed to her like the howling of the wind in the fir trees at home and she had tried to follow the sound.

"Fir trees! What nonsense! Do you think we live in a wood! Come and see the mess you have made!"

Heidi followed Fraulein Rottenmeier upstairs. She gazed in astonishment at the havoc she had created, for in her haste to get downstairs she had noticed nothing.

"You won't do this a second time," warned Fraulein Rottenmeier. "During lessons you will sit still and pay attention! And if you can't do that I will have to tie you to your chair. Do you understand?"

"Yes," said Heidi. "I shall be good now."

Sebastian and Tinette were called in to restore order

and the tutor went away because there could be no more lessons that day—there had not even been time for yawning!

Clara always rested in the afternoons, so Heidi was told she might do as she pleased. This suited her perfectly because there was something she very much wanted to do. But she needed assistance, and for this reason she posted herself in front of the dining-room door, right in the centre of the hall so that she would not miss the person to whom she wished to speak. It was not very long before Sebastian came upstairs carrying a large tray.

"Is there something the little fraulein wants?" inquired Sebastian, carrying the silver into the dining-room.

"How do you open a window, Sebastian?"

"Like this!" And he opened one of the large windows in the dining-room.

Heidi crossed over to the window but she was not tall enough to be able to see out.

"Here you are!" said Sebastian, bringing a high stool. "Now the little fraulein can see everything that is going on in the street down below."

Cheerfully Heidi climbed up and at last managed to see out of the window. Greatly disappointed, she withdrew her head almost at once. "But I can only see the stony street! Nothing else!" she said sadly. "If you go round the house what do you see on the other side, Sebastian?"

"Just the same!" he replied.

"But where have you to go to see over the whole valley?" she asked.

"Then you must climb a high tower or a church steeple, like that one with the golden ball. From there you can see ever so far."

At that, Heidi quickly jumped down from her stool and raced downstairs into the street. But it was not so easy as she had imagined. When she saw the steeple from the window it looked as though she only had to cross the street to reach it. But although she had walked right down the street she had not come to the steeple and she could not even see it any longer. She walked on and on. Many people passed but they all seemed to be in such a hurry that Heidi did not like to stop any of them to ask the way. Then Heidi saw a boy standing on the street corner with a barrel organ and, perched on his arm, a very strange-looking little animal. Heidi went forward and asked, "Where is the tower with the golden ball on the top?"

"Don't know!" answered the boy.

"Who can tell me, then?" asked Heidi again.

"Don't know."

"Don't you know of any church with a high steeple?"

"Yes, I know one!"

"Well, then, come and show it to me!"

"You show me first what you will give me for it!" said the boy, holding his hand out. Heidi searched in her pocket and found a pretty little card on which was printed a wreath of red roses. It was not easy to part with it for it had been given to her by Clara only that morning. But she longed to be able to look down over the green slopes into the valley. "There," said Heidi, "would you like this?"

The boy withdrew his hand and shook his head.

"What do you want, then?" asked Heidi, cheerfully putting away her little picture.

"Money," said the boy.

"I haven't got any now, but Clara will give me some later. How much do you want?"

"Twopence."

"Well, come along, then!"

They walked down a long street and on the way Heidi asked her companion what he was carrying on his back. He told her it was a barrel organ which played beautiful music when you turned the handle. All at once they found themselves in front of an old church with a high steeple. The boy stood still and pointed at it.

"But how can I get in?" asked Heidi when she saw that the doors were closed.

"Don't know," came the reply.

"Perhaps I could ring the bell as we do for Sebastian." Heidi had discovered a bell in the wall which she now pulled as hard as she could.

"When I go up you must wait here for me for I don't know my way back and you must show it to me."

"What will I get for it?"

"What do you want?"

"Another twopence."

They heard steps inside and the door creaked open. An old man appeared, looking first surprised and then angry when he saw the children. "How dare you ring the bell like that!" he shouted at them. "Can't you read the notice? 'Visitors wishing to go to the top of the tower, please ring!'"

The boy said nothing but pointed to Heidi.

"But that's just what I want!" said Heidi.

"Why do you want to go up there?" asked the caretaker. "Did somebody send you?"

"No," said Heidi. "I would just like to go up to the top and look down."

"Be off with you! And don't dare to try this trick on me again!" said the old man and was about to close the door; but Heidi grasped his coat and cried beseechingly, "Let me go up just once!"

The imploring look in Heidi's eyes made the old

man change his mind. He took her hand and said kindly, "If you really want it so much I will take you up."

The boy sat down on the stone steps and prepared to wait.

Together Heidi and the old man climbed many, many steps which became smaller and smaller as they went up, until at last, a very narrow little stair led up to the top of the tower. The caretaker lifted Heidi up to let her see out of the window. "Now you can look down," he said.

Heidi saw nothing but roofs, steeples and chimneys. She withdrew her head presently and said, very dispiritedly, "It is not at all as I expected."

"There! You see how a little one like you knows nothing about views. Now come down and never ring my bell again!"

The old man put Heidi back down on the floor and went ahead of her down the narrow stair. When the steps got broader they came to the caretaker's little room and beside it, underneath the sloping roof, stood a big basket. In front of it sat a big grey cat which snarled and spat because inside the basket lived her family and she wanted to warn everybody not to meddle with them. Heidi looked at her in amazement. She had never seen such a big cat. There were scores of mice in the old tower and the cat had no difficulty in catching half a dozen every day, for her kittens. The caretaker saw the look of delight on Heidi's face and said, "Come! She won't hurt you when I am here. You can still look at the kittens."

Heidi went over to the basket and exclaimed joyfully, "Oh, what sweet little kittens!"

"Would you like one?" asked the old man as he watched Heidi with amusement.

"For myself? To keep?" whispered Heidi, who could hardly believe her luck.

"Yes, you can have them all if you like," he said, thinking this would be a better way of getting rid of them than drowning.

Heidi was overjoyed. There was certainly plenty of room in the big house and how happy the kittens would make Clara!

"But how can I carry them away?" asked Heidi, picking some of them up, but the big cat sprang at her arm and hissed at her so fiercely that she shrank back.

"I will bring them to you if you will tell me the address," said the old man.

"Herr Sesemann's. On the door there is a dog's head with a gold ring in its mouth."

The caretaker did not need such a detailed description. He had been in the church for many years and knew every house in the district.

"I know the house."

"If only I could take one or two with me—one for me and one for Clara! May I ? "

"Yes! Take them."

Heidi's eyes shone with delight. She chose a white one and a tabby and put one into her right and one into her left pocket. Then they went downstairs.

The boy was still sitting on the steps outside. He jumped up when he saw Heidi and in a short time they reached the house. Heidi rang the bell and Sebastian opened the door. When he saw Heidi he hustled her inside.

"Quickly! Into the dining-room! They are all at table and Fraulein Rottenmeier looks like a loaded cannon. But why did you run away like that?"

Heidi went into the room. Fraulein Rottenmeier did not look up, Clara said nothing and it was an altogether uneasy atmosphere. When Heidi was seated

Fraulein Rottenmeier began in a very severe and solemn voice :

"Adelheid! I shall talk to you afterwards. I will only say now that you have behaved exceedingly badly, leaving the house without permission. Your conduct is unparalleled!"

"Miaow!" It sounded like an answer.

Now the lady's temper rose, "What Adelheid! You are rude as well as naughty! I warn you!"

"I didn't——" began Heidi. "Miaow! Miaow!"

Sebastian could conceal his amusement no longer and had to leave the room.

"That will do!" Fraulein Rottenmeier tried to say, but her voice cracked with excitement. "Get up and leave the room!"

Heidi, frightened, got up and tried to explain, "I really didn't—Miaow! Miaow!"

"But Heidi," Clara said reproachfully, "when you see it makes Fraulein Rottenmeier angry why do you go on saying ' Maiow?'"

"I didn't! It is the kittens!"

"What! Cats!" screamed Fraulein Rottenmeier. "Sebastian! Tinette! Find the horrid animals! Remove them at once!"

The lady rushed into the study and locked the door for she disliked cats more than anything.

Sebastian had to wait outside the door until his face was straight again. When he had served Heidi he had noticed the little kitten's head peeping out of her pocket. When at last he entered the room everything seemed quiet and peaceful again. Clara had the kittens on her lap and Heidi knelt beside her. Both played happily with the two tiny animals.

"Sebastian," said Clara. "You must help us to find a place for the kittens where Fraulein Rottenmeier will not find them, because she is afraid of them and wants to get rid of them. Where can we put them?"

"I shall see to that, Fraulein Clara," replied Sebastian willingly. "I shall prepare a nice bed in a basket and put it in a place where madam is not likely to go; rely on me!"

Much later Fraulein Rottenmeier opened the door an inch or two and called through the slit, "Are the horrid animals away?"

"Yes! Yes!" answered Sebastian, quietly collecting the kittens from Clara's lap and disappearing with them.

The lecture for Heidi was put off until the following day as Fraulein Rottenmeier felt too exhausted, and retired quietly. Clara and Heidi went cheerfully to bed, knowing that the kittens were all right.

CHAPTER 8

A Commotion in the House

━━━━━━━

THE FOLLOWING morning, shortly after Sebastian had admitted the tutor, the door bell rang again, so loudly this time that the butler thought the master himself had arrived home unexpectedly. He rushed downstairs and threw open the door, and there stood a little ragged boy with a barrel organ on his shoulder.

"What do you want?" asked Sebastian irritably. "I'll teach you to ring the bell like that! Be off with you!"

"I want to see Clara," the urchin replied.

"You cheeky little brat! Don't you know to say *Fraulein* Clara? What could you possibly have to see Fraulein Clara about?" stormed Sebastian.

"She owes me fourpence," said the boy.

"You must be insane! What makes you think Fraulein Clara lives here, anyway?"

"Yesterday I showed her the way for twopence; and back again; that was fourpence."

"You are telling a pack of lies! Fraulein Clara never goes out—she can't walk. Be off with you now before I take my boot to you!"

But the boy was not to be turned away so easily. He stood firm and repeated determinedly, "But I have seen her in the street and can tell you what she looks like. She has short, curly hair and she wears a brown dress. She talks different from us."

"Ho!" thought Sebastian. "So this is more mischief the little fraulein has been up to!" He chuckled to

66

himself as an idea occurred to him, then he said aloud, "Very well. Come with me, but wait outside the door until I call you, and when I let you into the room begin right away to play a tune on your barrel organ for the young lady. That will please her."

Sebastian knocked on the study door and went in. "There is a boy outside who says he has a message for Fraulein Clara," he announced.

This unexpected interruption to the lesson delighted Clara. "Let him come in at once!" she begged, turning to her tutor. "You see, he wants to speak to me particularly."

The boy entered, and at once started to play his organ according to Sebastian's instructions. Fraulein Rottenmeier was busy in the dining-room when the sound came to her ears. Was it in the street? Yet it seemed so much nearer! But who could be playing an organ in the study? And yet . . . She rushed into the study, and there, incredible as it seemed, there stood the ragged organ player. The tutor looked as though he were making an effort to speak, but failed. Clara and Heidi were listening happily.

"Stop! Stop at once!" commanded Fraulein Rottenmeier, but her voice was drowned by the music. She was walking towards the boy when suddenly on the floor between her feet she caught sight of a horrible, dark, crawling animal. It was a tortoise! At the sight of it, Fraulein Rottenmeier leaped into the air, shrieking at the top of her voice, "Sebastian! Sebastian!"

The organ player stopped abruptly. Sebastian stood behind the door, convulsed with laughter. At last he came in.

"Take them away! All of them! Boy, animal and all! At once, Sebastian!"

Sebastian dragged off the boy with the tortoise, at the same time putting something into his hand and whispering, "Fourpence for Fraulein Clara and fourpence for the music. You have done well!"

The door closed behind the little organ player, peace returned to the study and the lesson continued. This time Fraulein Rottenmeier remained in the room, grimly determined to prevent further incident.

Again a knock came to the study door and Sebastian appeared with the news that someone had brought a large basket to be delivered to Fraulein Clara. He carried in a covered basket and then disappeared.

"I think we will finish the lesson first," said Fraulein Rottenmeier, "and then we will see what is inside the basket."

Clara could not imagine what it could be and looked longingly at the basket. She broke off in the midst of her declensions to ask the tutor if she might have just one peep inside. The tutor frowned and was just about to refuse his permission when the lid of the basket lifted of its own accord and out jumped one, two, three, and then another two, and then several more kittens, and they all raced about the room in every direction. They climbed up on to Fraulein Rottenmeier's dress and scampered about her feet. They climbed up on Clara's chair, and, in fact, went into every corner of the room, scratching and maiowing. Clara cried delightedly, "Oh, look at them, Heidi! Aren't they sweet!"

Heidi raced about after them and the tutor, in a dilemma, moved uncomfortably from one foot to the other, at a complete loss to know what to do. At first, Fraulein Rottenmeier was too horror-stricken to utter a word, then she began to scream, "Tinette! Sebastian! Sebastian! Tinette!" She was terrified to move from her chair until Sebastian and Tinette appeared at last and removed the kittens.

There had been no yawning during lessons that day.

In the evening, Fraulein Rottenmeier held an inquiry into the affair. She summoned Sebastian and Tinette and it soon became evident that Heidi, on her excursion of the previous day, had been responsible for all these alarming occurrences. Fraulein Rottenmeier was pale with anger. She gave a sign for Sebastian and Tinette to withdraw, then she turned to Heidi who stood beside Clara's chair, not very sure of what crime she had been guilty.

"Adelheid," Fraulein Rottenmeier began in a stern voice, "I know of only one punishment which will make you aware of your frightful misconduct for you are nothing but a little barbarian. We shall see if a spell down in the dark cellar with the rats and black beetles will tame you a little so that you will know not to do such things in future."

Heidi listened in silence and was rather surprised at the threatened punishment for she had never been in such a cellar. The room which the grandfather called the cellar at home was a very pleasant place where the fresh cheese and milk were kept.

But Clara started to cry, sobbing, "No! No! Fraulein Rottenmeier! You must wait till Papa comes home. He said in his letter that he would come back soon and when he does I will tell him everything and he shall decide what is to be done with Heidi."

Fraulein Rottenmeier was obliged to agree and she got up and left the room, grumbling, "Well, Clara, I too will have something to say to Herr Sesemann."

Although a few days passed quietly after this, Fraulein Rottenmeier failed to regain her peace of mind. She was constantly aware of the disappointment that Heidi had been and of the fact that since her arrival the whole household had been upset. But Clara was very happy indeed. She was never bored now for during lessons something amusing was always happening. Instead of trying to learn the letters, Heidi would cry out, "Oh, it is shaped like a goat's horn!" or "It is like an eagle!" until the poor tutor would completely lose patience. Then, after lessons were over, in the late afternoon, Heidi would sit by Clara and tell her about the Alm and how much she wanted to go back. Indeed, She would talk about her old home until the longing to go back became so great that she would say, "I must go home again! To-morrow I must really go!" But Clara would persuade her to stay, saying, "Just wait until Papa comes home!" And Heidi would remember that each day she stayed meant that she could add another roll to her collection. Every night at supper she found a soft white roll on her plate and she would quietly slip it into her pocket. So she now had quite an amazing quantity of rolls to take back to the grandmother!

Every afternoon, while Clara rested, Heidi found herself alone and then she would sit by herself and think about the Alm. One day, the memory of the snow-capped peaks and the green valley made her feel so homesick that she hastily put the rolls into her red scarf, put on her little straw hat and started off for home. But she got no farther than the front door, for there stood Fraulein Rottenmeier, just returned from her walk. Her sharp eyes looked Heidi up and down. "What is the meaning of this? Didn't I forbid you to run about in the streets?"

"I wasn't going to run about, I just wanted to go home," explained Heidi, frightened.

"Wanted to go home, indeed! I wonder what Herr Sesemann would have to say to this? Running away from his beautiful house! What do you find wrong with it, I should like to know? Are you not treated better than you deserve? Have you ever in your life had such

H.   D a splendid place to live in or had so many servants to wait upon you? Have you?"

"No," said Heidi.

"I should think not," continued the lady. "You are an exceedingly ungrateful child who thinks of nothing but getting into mischief."

This rebuke was too much for Heidi and she began to pour out all the things that she had kept hidden for so long. "I only want to go home because Snowflake will be crying and the grandmother is waiting for me; and Goldfinch gets beaten when Goat Peter doesn't get part of my lunch. Here I can never watch the sun saying good night to the mountains, and if the great bird were to fly over Frankfurt he would croak even louder about so many people huddling together, gossiping, and not living in the mountains where it is so much nicer."

"Mercy! The child has gone out of her mind!" cried Fraulein Rottenmeier, rushing upstairs and colliding with Sebastian. "Take the unfortunate creature upstairs at once!" she called to him.

"What mischief have we been up to now, eh?" said Sebastian good-humouredly. Heidi stood trembling and frightened, and when Sebastian saw the distress on her little face he said kindly, "Now, now! Don't take it so much to heart! Cheer up and everything will be all right! Come! We'd better do as we were told and go upstairs."

Heidi looked such a picture of dejection as she slowly climbed the stairs that Sebastian felt really sorry for her. "Don't you give in!" he said encouragingly. "There's a brave little girl! Never a tear all the time she is with us and others at her age cry twelve times a day. And the kittens are so happy! You should just see them jumping about in the loft! Afterwards we shall go up and look at them, together, shall we?—when madam is not here."

Heidi nodded, but not very cheerfully, and disappeared into her room.

At supper Fraulein Rottenmeier did not speak but kept casting very odd glances in Heidi's direction as though she expected the child to do something extraordinary at any moment. But Heidi sat silently at the table, neither eating nor drinking although the roll had, as usual, disappeared quickly into her pocket.

Next morning, when the tutor arrived, Fraulein Rottenmeier took him into the dining-room and told him her worries about Heidi and of her attempt to go home the previous day. "I really think the child has gone mad," she concluded. The tutor managed to quieten her fears, explaining that Adelheid was perhaps a little strange but with careful handling and education the balance would soon be restored.

Fraulein Rottenmeier felt quite relieved after this conversation and during the afternoon she began to recall Heidi's outlandish appearance when she had prepared to set out on her journey. She decided that the child had better have one or two things from Clara's wardrobe before Herr Sesemann arrived. Clara was completely in favour of the plan and the lady went into Heidi's room to inspect her wardrobe. Very soon she returned, wearing an expression of complete disgust. "Adelheid!" she said. "I have never seen anything like it! In a wardrobe of all places, what do I find? Heaps of little rolls! Who ever heard of keeping bread in a wardrobe? Tinette! Go and remove all that stale bread from Heidi's wardrobe —and you can take away the old straw hat, too!"

"No! No!" screamed Heidi. "Not the hat! And the rolls are for Grandmother!" And she began to run after Tinette until Fraulein Rottenmeier stopped her.

"Stay just where you are!" she said. "All that rubbish must be thrown out."

Then Heidi threw herself into Clara's chair, crying in despair. "Now Grandmother won't get her rolls. She has taken them away!" and she sobbed as though her heart would break.

Clara was very much alarmed at this outburst and pleaded, "Heidi! Heidi! Don't cry! Listen to me! I will give you as many rolls as you want when you go home and they will be soft and fresh. Yours were quite stale. Don't cry any more, Heidi!"

It was a long time before Heidi could stop sobbing but Clara's promise had comforted her.

At supper, Heidi's eyes were still swollen with crying and when she looked at her roll she started to sob again; but with a great effort she managed to control herself for she knew that she had to be quiet at table. Whenever Sebastian came near he smiled at her encouragingly as if to say, "I will put everything right for you."

When it came time for Heidi to go to bed, what did she find under the bed-cover but her old hat! She hugged it with delight, knocking it more out of shape than ever; then she wrapped it in a handkerchief and put it right at the back of the wardrobe. Sebastian had seen Tinette with the hat and had taken it from her quickly, saying, "It's all right. I shall dispose of this." This had been the reason for all the nods and smiles which Sebastian had given Heidi at supper.

CHAPTER 9

News from the Master

~~~~~~~~

A FEW DAYS later there was great excitement in the house because Herr Sesemann had returned. Sebastian and Tinette were kept busy carrying up parcels and suitcases from the carriage. They were packed with all sorts of exciting presents which Clara's father was in the habit of bringing back from his travels.

It was late afternoon when Herr Sesemann arrived and he came straight into the study where Clara and Heidi were sitting together. Father and daughter greeted each other affectionately, then Herr Sesemann held out his hand to Heidi and said kindly, "And this is our little Swiss girl? Come and shake hands with me! That's right! Now, Clara, you must allow me to go and have something to eat. I have had nothing since breakfast. Later I shall see you again and show you all the things I have brought home."

In the dining-room he found Fraulein Rottenmeier inspecting the table which was laid for dinner. Herr Sesemann sat down and Fraulein Rottenmeier, looking the picture of gloom, took her place opposite.

"What is the matter, Fraulein Rottenmeier?" asked Herr Sesemann. "You look very dismal. Have you had a stroke of bad luck? Clara seems to be cheerful enough. What is wrong?"

With a very long face, the lady began, "Herr Sesemann, we have been completely deceived—and it concerns Clara."

"In what way?" Herr Sesemann asked calmly.

"You know we decided that Clara should have a companion, and as I knew you were anxious to have a nicely brought up girl, I thought of a little Swiss girl of whom I had heard a great deal. But I have been terribly cheated. Completely taken in! Really shockingly!"

"But what is so shocking? I see nothing shocking in the child," remarked Herr Sesemann, still completely unperturbed.

"Oh, if you only knew the type of people—and the animals!—this creature has brought into your house! The tutor can tell you all about it."

"Animals? What am I to understand from that, Fraulein Rottenmeier?"

"Herr Sesemann, it is beyond *my* understanding! Her whole behaviour would be beyond comprehension were it not for one thing. She has spells of mental disturbance!" concluded Fraulein Rottenmeier with conviction.

Up till now, Herr Sesemann had not thought the affair of any great importance; but mental disturbance! That could very easily have a harmful effect on his little daughter.

He looked quickly at Fraulein Rottenmeier as though to assure himself that it was not she who was the victim of a troubled mind. Just then, the door opened and the tutor entered.

"Ah, here is our tutor! Perhaps he can clear this matter up for us," Herr Sesemann exclaimed. "Come, sit down and have a cup of coffee with us," he said, addressing the tutor. "No need for ceremony. Now tell me what is wrong with this child who has come to be a companion to my daughter. What's this about her bringing animals into the house, and about her mental faculties?"

The tutor began in his usual roundabout way, "Since you ask me for my opinion about this young girl, Herr

Sesemann, I should like to direct your attention to the fact that, although there may be a lack of development, caused by more or less neglected education, or rather by somewhat delayed tuition, on the one hand, there is, on the other hand, I think we must admit, a certain benefit to be gained from such a solitary life in the mountains, and we must consider——"

"My dear friend," interrupted Herr Sesemann, "you take too much trouble. Tell me, did her bringing animals to the house alarm you too, and what is your opinion of her as a companion for my little daughter?"

"I have no wish to say anything against the young girl," the tutor began again. "If on the one hand there is a certain inexperience of social custom, owing to the somewhat uncivilised life she led up to the time she came to Frankfurt, on the other hand she has gifts not to be overlooked, and if carefully led——"

"My dear sir, you must please excuse me now. I must speak to my daughter." And with these words Herr Sesemann quickly left the room.

In the study, he sat down beside his little girl and turning to Heidi said, "Listen, little one, will you go and fetch me—ah—fetch me——" Herr Sesemann wanted the child out of the room but was having difficulty in thinking up an excuse. "Fetch me a glass of water?"

Heidi disappeared at once.

"And now, my dear Clara," said Herr Sesemann, pulling his chair closer and taking his daughter's hand, "tell me quite frankly, what kind of animals did your little friend bring into the house? And what makes Fraulein Rottenmeier think that she is sometimes not quite right in her mind?"

Clara had no difficulty in explaining. She told her father the story of the tortoise and the kittens and explained all the remarks which Fraulein Rottenmeier had thought so odd, and which seemed to upset her so much.

Herr Sesemann laughed heartily. "Well, then, you don't want me to send the child home, Clara? You are not tired of her?" asked her father.

"No! No! Papa. Please don't!" exclaimed Clara in alarm. "The time has passed so quickly since Heidi came. Something happens every day, and it used to be so dull. And she always has so much to tell me."

"Very well, then. Ah! Here is our little friend! Have you brought me nice fresh water?" Herr Sesemann asked as Heidi handed him the glass.

"Yes. It is fresh from the pump," answered Heidi.

"Did you go yourself to the pump, Heidi?" asked Clara.

"Yes, but I had to go a long way because at the first pump there were ever so many people and at the second there were just as many. Then I went into another street and got the water there. The gentleman with the white hair sends his kind regards to Herr Sesemann."

"Well, that was a long expedition," laughed Herr Sesemann. "And who is this gentleman?"

"As he was passing the pump he stopped and said, 'Since you have got a glass would you mind giving me a drink? To whom are you taking the glass of water?' And I said, 'To Herr Sesemann.' And he laughed and gave me the message for you and said he hoped Herr Sesemann would enjoy the water."

"And what did this gentleman look like who sends me so many good wishes?" asked Herr Sesemann.

"He wore a thick gold chain with a big red stone hanging from it; and the top of his stick was a horse's head."

"That is our old friend, the doctor," cried Clara and

her father at the same instant. Herr Sesemann smiled to himself as he wondered what their friend would think of the new way in which the Sesemanns went about quenching their thirst.

That very evening, he told Fraulein Rottenmeier that Heidi would remain; that he found the child perfectly normal and that his daughter preferred her company to any other. "I am anxious, therefore," said Herr Sesemann emphatically, "that this child should always be treated in a friendly way and that her little peculiarities should not be treated as crimes. And, by the way, if you find difficulty in managing the child there is a prospect that you will be relieved of this duty. I am expecting my mother very soon for a long visit, and, as you know, she gets along with everybody, Fraulein Rottenmeier," he concluded pointedly.

"Yes, I know, Herr Sesemann," said Fraulein Rottenmeier rather sourly.

Herr Sesemann remained only a short time at home and after a fortnight he set off for Paris, comforting his little daughter with the prospect of the arrival of her grandmother in a day or two.

On the day after Herr Sesemann's departure, a letter came announcing Frau Sesemann's arrival on the following day. Clara was overjoyed and talked so much about her grandmother that Heidi, too, called her Grandmamma. Fraulein Rottenmeier gave her a very disapproving look which did not impress Heidi very much since the lady was always finding fault with her in any case.

Later, when Heidi was going to her bedroom, Frauelin Rottenmeier took her into her own room and instructed her that she should never address Frau Sesemann as Grandmamma but always as 'madam'. "Do you understand?" she asked.

Heidi really did not understand at all why she should call the lady by this title but Fraulein Rottenmeier's face wore such a severe expression as she spoke that Heidi did not dare ask for an explanation.

CHAPTER 10

Another Grandmother

~~~~~~~~~

THE FOLLOWING evening great preparations were afoot in the Sesemann house and presently there was the sound of a carriage stopping at the front door. Sebastian and Tinette rushed downstairs and Fraulein Rottenmeier followed, but slowly and with dignity. She knew that she would have to be there to welcome Frau Sesemann. Heidi, who had been ordered to wait in her room until she was called, sat in a corner and repeated over and over again to herself the little speech which she had been instructed to address to Frau Sesemann.

Before very long Tinette came to call her. Putting her head round the door, she announced in her usual saucy manner, "You're to go into the study."

Heidi made her way to the study, still turning the words over in her mind and still hardly able to believe that she should address any one in the peculiar way Fraulein Rottenmeier had told her. As she opened the door, the grandmother said in a kind voice, "Ah, here is the child! Come here and let me look at you!"

Heidi approached, and said very distinctly in her clear voice, "Good evening, madam!"

"Well," said the grandmother, laughing. "Is that how you address people on the Alm?"

"No. At home nobody has a name like that," said Heidi gravely.

"Neither do they here!" said the grandmother, still smiling, and patted Heidi's cheek. " When I am with children I am always Grandmamma. Can you remember that?"

"Yes, very well," Heidi assured her, "because that's what I used to say."

"I understand," said the grandmother, shaking her head a little. She looked more closely at Heidi and Heidi's steady, serious eyes looked back at her eagerly, for there was a warmth about the old woman which attracted the child. Heidi gazed entranced at the beautiful white hair which was adorned with a lacy frill, ending in two broad ribbons which floated gently about the grandmother's head as though blown by a soft breeze.

"And what is your name, child?"

"It is really Heidi, but if you call me Adelheid I shall try to remember——" Heidi stopped guiltily, remembering that sometimes she failed to answer when Fraulein Rottenmeier called her by this name. Just at that, Fraulein Rottenmeier entered.

"Frau Sesemann will agree that I had to choose a name which one could pronounce, and, of course, on account of the servants——"

"Very correct, I have no doubt, Rottenmeier," replied Frau Sesemann, "but if the child is called Heidi and is accustomed to that name, I shall call her by it; so that's settled."

Fraulein Rottenmeier found it very embarrassing to be called by her surname but since the grandmother would have her own way there was nothing she could do about it. She was a very alert old lady and had her wits about her, and she very soon knew exactly what was going on in the house.

The following afternoon, after sitting by Clara's bed until she fell asleep, Frau Sesemann went upstairs and knocked at Fraulein Rottenmeier's door. Fraulein Rottenmeier looked startled at this unexpected visit.

"Where is the Heidi child and what is she doing, I should like to know," said Frau Sesemann, coming straight to the point.

"She is in her room where she could find something useful to do if she had the slightest inclination," replied Fraulein Rottenmeier. "But if Frau Sesemann only knew the queer things she imagines and does—I can hardly bring myself to talk of them."

"And so would I, if I were in her place, I don't doubt. Tell the little one to come to my room. I have some nice books to give her."

"But that's just it!" replied Fraulein Rottenmeier, throwing up her hands in despair. "Of what use are books to her? She does not even know the alphabet yet! It is quite impossible to teach her anything. The tutor will tell you so himself. If he didn't have the patience of a saint he would have given up trying to teach her long ago."

"Well, that is strange. The child does not strike me as being stupid," said Frau Sesemann shortly. "Now go and fetch her. She can look at the pictures for the time being."

Fraulein Rottenmeier was about to say more but Frau Sesemann turned and went quickly into her room.

Heidi was greatly delighted with the beautiful coloured pictures in the books which the grandmother had brought. Suddenly she cried aloud as the grandmother turned a page, and when the old lady looked at the child she saw that tears were streaming down her cheeks. She looked at once at the picture. It depicted a beautiful green pasture with all sorts of animals grazing. In the midst, the shepherd leant upon his stick and looked happily at his flock. Everything was bathed in a golden light for the sun was just setting on the far horizon.

The grandmother took Heidi's hand gently. "Come, come, child! Don't cry! It has reminded you of something, perhaps. But look, there is a beautiful story about it and I am going to tell it to you to-night. There are many beautiful stories in this book which can be read over and over again. Come now, we must have a chat, so dry your tears and stand in front of me so that I can look at you. That's right. Now we are happy again."

Heidi tried very hard to stop sobbing and when at last she succeeded the grandmother said, "Now I want you to tell me something, child. How are you getting on with your lessons? Do you like them? Are you doing well?"

"Oh, no!" answered Heidi with a sigh. "But I knew it would be impossible."

"What is impossible, Heidi? What do you mean?"

"To learn to read. It is too difficult."

"Well I never! And who told you this?"

"Peter did, and he knows for he has tried and tried but he can't learn. It is too difficult."

"What a boy Peter must be! But listen to me, Heidi. We must never believe what the 'Peters' say but try for ourselves. I am sure you have never paid enough attention to the tutor or looked properly at the letters."

"It is no use," said Heidi with a great sigh of resignation.

"Now, Heidi. Listen to what I say! You have not been able to learn to read because you believed what Peter said. Now you must believe what I say when I tell you that you can learn to read like many other children who are like you and not like Peter, and in a very short time. First you must know what happens when you are able to read. Do you see the Shepherd on the beautiful green pasture? Well, as soon as you can read you shall have the book for your own and then you will know the whole story just as if someone were to tell it to you—what the shepherd did with his sheep and goats and the wonderful things that happened to him. Wouldn't you like to know all that, Heidi?"

Heidi had been listening with keen attention and now exclaimed with sparkling eyes, "Oh, if only I could read already!"

"You will learn in no time—I can see that, Heidi. But now we must go to Clara. Come, we will take the books with us!"

The grandmother took Heidi's hand and they went together into the study.

From the day Heidi had tried to go home and Fraulein Rottenmeier had scolded her for being so wicked and ungrateful a change had come over the child. She knew now that she could not go home whenever she liked, as Aunt Dete had told her, but that she had to stay in Frankfurt for a long time, maybe for ever. She also understood that Herr Sesemann would think her very ungrateful, and Clara and the grandmother, too, if she again showed signs of wanting to leave. So there was nobody to whom she could reveal how homesick she was for she could not face giving the grandmother, who was so kind to her, cause to be angry as Fraulein Rottenmeier had been.

But the strain of keeping all this to herself became almost more than she could bear. She lost her appetite and every day grew paler and paler. At night she would lie awake for a long time, for as soon as she was alone with everything quiet around her, she would see again in her thoughts the Alm and the sunshine and the flowers, and when at last she fell asleep she would see in her dreams the red summits of the crags and the crimson snowfield in the evening sun. Awakening in the morning she wanted to run out happily into the sun—but she soon realised that she was in the big bed at Frankfurt, far, far away from home. Then Heidi would weep long and quietly, her head pressed into the pillow so that no one could hear.

Heidi's unhappiness did not escape the grandmother. She waited a few days to see if there might be a change. But as Heidi remained subdued and when she noticed that often in the early morning the child looked as though she had been crying, the grandmother took her, one day, into her room and said lovingly, "Now tell me, Heidi, what is the matter? Are you worrying about something?"

But not for the world would Heidi show ingratitude to the grandmother who had been so kind, so she replied:

"Please, I cannot tell you."

"Could you tell Clara, then?"

"Oh, no! Nobody," said Heidi, looking so pitiful that the grandmother was filled with compassion.

"Come here, little one, and I will tell you something. If one is in trouble and can't speak about it to any one then one tells it to God who is in Heaven and prays to Him for help because he is able to take away all our troubles. Do you know that? Do you pray every night to your Heavenly Father and thank Him for all he has done for you and ask Him to keep you from harm?"

"Oh, no! I never do that," answered Heidi.

"Have you never prayed, Heidi? Don't you know what it is?"

"Sometimes I used to pray with the first grandmother but it is a long time ago and I have forgotten it."

"You see, Heidi, because you have nobody to help you, you are unhappy. Think how wonderful it is when our hearts are heavy with sadness, to be able to go any moment to God and tell Him everything and ask Him for help when no one else can give it. He is always able to help and can give us what makes us happy again."

A gleam of joy came into Heidi's eyes, "May I tell Him everything?"

"Everything, Heidi. Everything."

Heidi drew away the hand which the grandmother held affectionately and asked hastily, "May I go?"

"Certainly, certainly!" answered the grandmother and Heidi ran off to her room. She sat down on her little stool, folded her hands and told God about everything that made her so unhappy and begged Him with all her heart to let her go home to the grandfather

A little more than a week after this the tutor asked to see Frau Sesemann as he had something very remarkable to tell her. When he was shown into her room Frau Sesemann held out her hand, saying, "I am pleased to see you. Sit down, won't you? Now tell me why you wish to see me. I hope it is not a complaint."

"On the contrary, madam," the tutor began. "Something has occurred—something which I did not expect. In the light of all my previous experience it was an impossibility and yet it really has happened. It is like a miracle. Contrary to all I had expected——"

"Am I to understand that the child, Heidi, has learned to read after all?" Frau Sesemann guessed.

Speechless with surprise the tutor looked at her.

"It is indeed nothing short of a miracle. In spite of my painstaking explanations, she never seemed to be able to learn the alphabet, and now she has learnt it with such rapidity—overnight, so to say—and so correctly! It is most unusual with a beginner."

"Life is full of miracles," Frau Sesemann smiled. "Of course, there might be such a happy coincidence as a fresh zeal for learning and a new method of teaching. Now we must be glad the child has made such a good beginning and hope for her future progress."

After she had seen the tutor to the door, she went straight to the study to make sure of the good news. Sure enough, Heidi was seated beside Clara and was reading a story to her with great eagerness, evidently surprised herself to find the black letters turning into real people and exciting adventures.

That same evening, at the dinner table, Heidi found by her plate the big book with the lovely pictures and when she looked questioningly at the grandmother the old lady nodded her confirmation, "Yes, it is yours, now."

"Always? Even when I go home?" asked Heidi, flushed with happiness.

"Of course, for ever!" assured the grandmother. "To-morrow we shall start to read it."

"But you are not going home yet, Heidi," Clara put in. "Not for many years. I want you to stay with me, especially when Grandmother goes away."

Before she went to bed, Heidi looked at her book, and from that day on, her greatest pleasure was to read over and over again the stories which belonged to the beautiful pictures.

When, in the evening, the grandmother said, "Now Heidi will read to us," the child was delighted and when she read aloud, the stories seemed to be still more beautiful and interesting. The picture she liked best was the one with the green pasture and the shepherd leaning happily on his crook. He was tending his father's fine flock. But the next picture showed how the shepherd had run away from home and had to look after a herd of swine. He had grown quite thin for all he had to eat was husks. In this picture, the sun did not shine so golden and the land was grey and misty. But then there was still another picture to this story. In it the old father was running with outstretched arms to meet his returning and repentant son, welcoming him as he approached timidly, tired and dirty and dressed in rags. This was Heidi's favourite story which she read again and again without ever tiring of hearing the grandmother's explanations of the meaning of the story. There were many other beautiful tales in the book and with reading and studying the pictures the days passed quickly and the time came for the grandmother's departure.

CHAPTER 11

Heidi Learns a Great Deal

~~~~~~

Every afternoon during her visit, the grandmother sat beside Clara for a time while she was resting, and afterwards she would call Heidi into her room and would talk to her and keep her occupied in all sorts of ways. The grandmother had pretty little dolls and showed Heidi how to make little dresses and coats for them so that without knowing it Heidi had learnt to sew. Since Heidi could now read she was allowed to read aloud to the grandmother and this she enjoyed very much, growing more fond of the stories the more she read them. But still, Heidi never looked really happy and her sparkling eyes were never as bright as before.

One afternoon during the last week of the grandmother's visit, when Heidi was paying her customary afternoon call the grandmother asked, "Tell me, child, why is it you are not happy? Is there still the same grief in your heart?"

"Yes," Heidi nodded.

"Have you told God about it?"

"Yes."

"And do you say your prayers every day so that all will be well and you will be happy again?"

"Oh, no. I don't pray at all now."

"What is this, Heidi? Why don't you pray any more?"

"It is no use. God does not listen, and I can understand it; when there are so many people in Frankfurt all praying to Him He cannot possibly listen to them all. He certainly has not heard me."

"What makes you so sure, Heidi?"

"I have prayed for the same thing every day for weeks and weeks and God has never done it."

"Oh, Heidi! That is not the way in which to think of Him. You see, God is our Heavenly Father and always knows what is best for us, even when we ourselves do not. If we ask for something which is not good for us He does not grant it but instead gives us the thing that is best for us. If we go on praying earnestly and never run away or lose faith our prayers will be answered. You see, Heidi, what you asked for was not good for you just at the moment. God has certainly heard you. He can hear every one at the same time because He is God and not a human being like you or me. And because He knows what is good for you He says, 'Yes, Heidi shall have what she wants but only when it is good for her; because if I give her what she wants right away and then, by and by, she sees that it would have been better for her not to have had her own way, she will say, 'If only God had not given me what I asked for! It is not so good as I thought.' Since God watched over you, you should have trusted in Him, come with everything to Him and prayed every day, but you ran away, stopped praying and forgot all about Him!

"But you see, when someone behaves like you so that God never hears his voice among those who pray, He lets him go his own way. And when he gets into trouble and then complains, 'There is no one to help me!' God says, 'Why did you run away from Me? I cannot help you when you run away.' Do you want that, Heidi? Or would you rather go and ask Him to forgive you for running away, and pray to Him every day and trust that He will make everything right for you and that you will be happy again?"

Every word the grandmother said had touched the child's heart and she said repentantly, "At once I will ask God to forgive me and I will never forget Him again."

"That is a good child. He will help you at the right moment, never fear!" And Heidi ran to her room and prayed to God to forgive her and asked Him not to forget her.

It was a sad time for Clara and Heidi when the day of the grandmother's departure arrived, but the old lady insisted on making it quite a party so that they would not think too much about her going. After the grandmother had driven off in her carriage the house seemed very empty and silent and Clara and Heidi felt quite lost.

The next day, when the children sat together in the afternoon, Heidi suggested to Clara that she should read aloud to her every afternoon. Clara was very pleased with this idea and Heidi began with great enthusiasm. But the first story turned out to be about a dying grandmother and Heidi, who took all the stories very seriously and believed every word was true, at once thought that it was the grandmother on the Alm who was dead and burst into tears. Clara tried to explain that the story was about a quite different grandmother, but the idea that such a thing could happen had entered Heidi's mind and she realised with a great shock that the grandmother and the grandfather also might die while she was so far away and if she did not go home for a very long time everything on the Alm might be silent and dead and she would be all alone and would never see her dear ones again. And these sad thoughts made her sob the louder.

In the midst of Clara's explanation Fraulein Rottenmeier had entered the room and as Heidi still continued to sob she burst out impatiently, "Adelheid! That will do! I warn you, if you continue to give way to these outbursts whenever you read I will take the book away from you for good."

Heidi turned pale at such a thought. The book was her most treasured possession. Hurriedly she dried her tears. The stratagem had worked all right. No matter what the story, Heidi never cried again. But sometimes it was so difficult to keep back the tears that Clara would say, "Heidi, what terrible faces you are making!" But grimaces made no noise and did not attract Fraulein Rottenmeier's attention.

Heidi began to lose her appetite again and grew so pale and thin that Sebastian was extremely perturbed when she refused to take any of the delicious food which he served. Often he would whisper encouragingly as he held out a dish, "Take a little of this, Fraulein Heidi! It is so good! No, not like that! A heaped spoonful, and another one!" and other pieces of fatherly advice. But it was no use. Heidi hardly ate anything and as she lay in bed at night she would begin to think about home and what might be happening there, and she would turn her face into her pillow so that no one would hear, and cry as though her heart would break.

The days went by and Heidi could hardly tell whether it were winter or summer, for all she ever saw of the outside world was the same grey walls and roofs. She was only allowed out when Clara was well enough to go for a short drive (which never took them farther than the neighbouring streets) and never had a glimpse of grass or flowers, let alone fir trees and mountains. Heidi's longing for the beautiful, remembered things grew every day so that she could not speak or think of them without her eyes filling with tears.

Autumn and winter passed and the spring sun shone on the white walls of the house opposite, and Heidi knew it would soon be the time when Peter climbed up to the Alm with his goats, the flowers glittered in the sunshine and in the evening the mountains turned to crimson in the setting sun. Heidi would sit in her lonely little room and press her palms into her eyes so that she would not be able to see the sunshine striking the wall, and so she sat, silently struggling against her homesickness until she heard Clara's voice calling her.

CHAPTER 12

The House is Haunted

~~~~~~~~

FOR SOME TIME, very strange things had been happening in the house. Every morning when the servants came down they found the front door wide open. During the first few days when this had happened all the rooms in the house were carefully searched for signs of burglary, but nothing was missing. At night every care was taken. The door was carefully locked and bolted, and to make it even more secure the wooden bar was put across. But all these precautions were of no avail; in the morning, the servants would again find the door wide open. At last John and Sebastian plucked up courage and promised to sit up all night in the room off the hall and watch to see what took place. Fraulein Rottenmeier, thinking they should be armed against any intruders, got out two of Herr Sesemann's pistols, and brought up a bottle of wine from the cellar with which the watchers might fortify their courage.

On the appointed night, the two installed themselves in the downstairs room and at once felt in need of a little stimulant. At first the wine made them very talkative, and by and by very sleepy, so they both leaned back in their arm-chairs and fell fast asleep. Sebastian awoke as the old church clock struck midnight. He called to his companion but John remained fast asleep. Sebastian did not go to sleep again but sat uneasily in the quietness of the night, only now and then giving John a quiet poke to see if he were awake. The clock struck the hour and John awoke with a start. He jumped to his feet and with a great show of courage said, "Now, Sebastian, we had better go outside and see what is going on. You aren't feeling scared, are you? Come on! I'll go first."

John opened the door wide and stepped into the hall. A sudden draught put out the light which he carried and he turned quickly, pushing against Sebastian, and stumbled back into the room, slamming the door and turning the key in the lock with feverish haste. Then he relit the candle. Sebastian did not know what to make of this odd behaviour and turned a puzzled look on John. In the light of the candle he saw that John was as white as a sheet and trembled all over. "What is it?" Sebastian asked hurriedly. "What did you see?"

"The door wide open," gasped John, "and on the stairs, a white figure—then, poof! and it was gone."

Sebastian shuddered with horror and felt as though his knees were going to give way. For the rest of the night the two sat close together and did not move again until the morning light came streaming through the window and the sound of passers-by came from the street. Then they went out and closed the front door and made their way upstairs to tell their story to Fraulein Rottenmeier. Straight away, she wrote a long letter to Herr Sesemann, telling him he would have to return at once as every one in the house now went in fear of his life and there was no knowing what the dreadful consequences of these incidents might be. But Herr Sesemann replied that it was impossible for him to return home just then, and altogether treated the affair very lightly.

Fraulein Rottenmeier was beginning to feel that she had had quite enough of this particular worry. She had never told the children of the apparition for fear of upsetting them, but now she had an idea. In a hushed voice and with much colourful detail, she told them of the nightly visitations. The story so frightened Clara that she began to scream for her father to come home. She was in such a state of fright that she would not be left alone for a minute. Fraulein Rottenmeier wrote another letter to Herr Sesemann saying she would not answer for the serious consequences the mysterious occurrences might have on his daughter's delicate constitution. This had the desired effect. Two days later Herr Sesemann came home. Clara was overjoyed to see him, and when he saw in what good spirits she was, a look of great relief spread over his features.

"And how is the ghost behaving?" he asked Fraulein Rottenmeier with a twinkle in his eye.

"It is no joke," she replied tartly. "I am sure by to-morrow Herr Sesemann will no longer consider it a laughing matter."

"Well, we shall see," replied Herr Sesemann. "Now send Sebastian to me."

Herr Sesemann knew that Sebastian and Fraulein Rottenmeier were not always on the best of terms and he had his own ideas as to the cause of the disturbances.

"Now, Sebastian," he said, "tell me frankly. Have you been playing ghosts to tease Fraulein Rottenmeier?"

"On my honour, sir, no!" replied Sebastian with unmistakable sincerity. "Please don't think that! I have been feeling very uncomfortable myself about this thing."

"Well, if that is so, I will have to show you and the brave John how ghosts look in the daylight. You should be ashamed of yourself, Sebastian, a big strong fellow like you running away from a ghost! But now go at once to my old friend Dr. Classen. Give him my kind regards and ask him to come here to-night at nine o'clock. Tell him I have come specially from Paris to consult him and will he make his arrangements to spend the night here. Do you understand?"

Promptly at nine o'clock the doctor arrived; a grey-haired man with bright, kindly eyes. At first he looked a little worried but presently he burst out laughing. "Well, well! For a patient with whom I am to sit up all night you don't look too bad."

"Not so hasty, my friend. Wait until I tell you this. There's a ghost in the house! This place is haunted!"

The doctor laughed uproariously.

"That's a fine way of showing your sympathy I must say," Herr Sesemann continued. "It's a pity my friend Rottenmeier can't enjoy it. She is convinced that some ancient member of the family is prowling about the house."

"And how did she make his acquaintance?" asked the doctor, still chuckling.

When the doctor had heard the whole story the two gentlemen went downstairs to the room where Sebastian and John had kept watch. There they settled themselves comfortably in arm-chairs and smoked and chatted together with such enjoyment that in what seemed no time at all they heard the clock strike twelve.

"The ghost seems to have got wind of us and does not choose to come to-night," said the doctor.

"Hold on! It usually comes before one o'clock," replied his friend.

They resumed their conversation and until one o'clock struck there was not a sound to be heard. Then suddenly the doctor lifted a finger.

"Hush, Sesemann. Don't you hear something?"

They both listened and heard distinctly the bar on the door being softly pushed aside, the key turning in the lock and the door opening. Herr Sesemann seized one of the pistols which lay ready on the table.

"You are not afraid are you?" whispered the doctor.

"As well to be careful," Herr Sesemann replied, picking

up the lamp. The doctor took the other pistol and together they stepped out into the hall.

Moonlight streamed through the open door and fell on a white figure which stood motionless on the threshold.

"Who is there?" the doctor demanded loudly, his voice echoing through the hall. As both gentlemen advanced towards the figure it turned and gave a little cry. In her little white nightgown and with her bare feet, Heidi stood there trembling and blinking at the light and the weapons pointed in her direction.

The gentlemen exchanged surprised glances.

"Well, if it isn't the little water-carrier!" said the doctor.

"Child, what does this mean?" asked Herr Sesemann. "Why have you come downstairs?"

Pale and trembling, Heidi stood before him. "I don't know," she whispered.

Then the doctor intervened. "Sesemann, this is something I shall have to deal with. Go and sit by the fire while I take the child up to bed."

The doctor put down his revolver and taking the child in his arms he carried her upstairs, and laying her on her bed he covered her carefully with the quilt. Then he sat on the edge of the bed, and taking her hand, he said kindly, "Everything is all right now. Tell me where you wanted to go."

"I didn't want to go at all," said Heidi. "I didn't know I was going but suddenly I was there."

"Were you dreaming about something?"

"Yes, I dream every night and it is always the same. I think I am with Grandfather and outside I hear the fir trees rustling and I think how beautifully the stars will be shining and I run quickly and open the door of the cottage. But when I awake I am still in Frankfurt."

Heidi struggled to swallow the lump which rose in her throat.

"And have you a pain anywhere? In your head or in your back?"

"No. Only a feeling as if there were a big stone here."

"As though you had eaten something and it would not go down?"

"No, not like that. But so heavy that it makes me want to cry and cry."

"I see, and then you have a good cry?"

"Oh, no, I mustn't. Fraulein Rottenmeier doesn't allow it."

"Then you just swallow hard, is that it? But you like being in Frankfurt, don't you?"

"Yes," said Heidi in a flat voice which made it sound more like 'no.'

"And where did you live when you were with your grandfather?"

"Always on the Alm."

"And wasn't that rather dull?"

"Oh, no, it was beautiful. It was so beautiful——" Heidi could not go on. Remembrance of the past, the recent excitement and the long-suppressed weeping overwhelmed the child. Tears gushed from her eyes and her little body was shaken with sobs. The doctor rose. Gently he laid Heidi's head on the pillow. "Cry a little. It will do no harm, and then sleep. To-morrow everything will be all right."

The doctor went downstairs and joined his friend. He lowered himself into the opposite arm-chair and looked across at him gravely. "Sesemann, your little protégé is a sleep-walker. Every night, without knowing it, she has been opening the front door and alarming your staff. The child is pining away with homesickness.

Didn't you see how pathetically thin she is? Now there is only one remedy and that is to send her back home at once. My advice is that the child should travel home to-morrow."

Herr Sesemann got up in a great state of agitation and strode up and down the room. "Ill! Homesick! Wasting away! In my house! And nobody seems to have noticed it! And you, doctor, suggest that I should send her back home in that pathetic state. No, doctor, I cannot do it. You take the child in hand and restore her to health; then I shall send her home if she wants to go."

"Sesemann," said the doctor, "consider! This is not an illness that can be cured with pills and powders. The child does not have a strong constitution but if she gets back home to the mountain air she will very quickly recover; if not—wouldn't you rather send the child back ill than not at all?"

Such blunt words alarmed Herr Sesemann and he agreed at once. "Well, if you think that is the only way then we must act at once." They discussed the matter further and after a while the doctor took his leave. When the master of the house opened the door the bright morning light shone in.

CHAPTER 13

Back to the Alm

~~~~~~~~

IN GREAT AGITATION, Herr Sesemann went upstairs to Fraulein Rottenmeier's room. His loud rap on the door awakened the lady and she was startled to hear him say, "Come down to the dining-room quickly, please! We must make preparations for a journey."

Fraulein Rottenmeier had never before been obliged to get up so early. It was only half-past four in the morning. What could possibly have happened? She was so flustered that she could hardly manage to dress. Herr Sesemann proceeded to rouse the whole staff and his urgent cries convinced them that the ghost had attacked the master and he needed their help. But, to their surprise, they found him walking up and down in the dining-room and not looking at all terrified. John was ordered to get the horses and carriage ready; Tinette had to wake Heidi and help her to dress.

At last Fraulein Rottenmeier was ready and came downstairs. Herr Sesemann instructed her to pack a trunk with the Swiss child's belongings and to add one or two things of Clara's so that the child would have some decent clothes to go home with. All this had to be done at once, Herr Sesemann insisted.

Poor Fraulein Rottenmeier stared in bewilderment at Herr Sesemann. She had expected to hear a hair-raising account of an encounter with a ghost and instead she was being given these practical instructions. Unable to believe her ears, she waited silently for Herr Sesemann to say something further; but he had no time for lengthy explanations and bustled off to Clara's room, leaving her standing there. He found Clara lying awake, wondering what could be the cause of such an upheaval in the house. Sitting beside her bed, her father told her all that had happened; about the doctor's verdict and how they had decided to send Heidi home again at once.

Clara was distressed and made all sorts of suggestions for keeping Heidi with her, but her father remained firm, promising that if she were a good girl and did not make a fuss he would take her to Switzerland the following year.

Herr Sesemann told Sebastian that he would have to accompany the child on her journey, the first day as far as Basle and the next day to her destination. He would be furnished with an explanatory letter to the grandfather, after presenting which he could return at once.

"But the main thing is this, Sebastian," concluded Herr Sesemann, "and I want you to see it is carried out. On this card I have written the name of the hotel in Basle. Show it to the manager and you will be given accommodation for the child and yourself. Go into the child's room and see that the windows are securely fastened, and when she has gone to bed, lock the door from the outside, for the child is a sleep-walker."

"Ah, so that was the ghost! I understand!" exclaimed Sebastian in great surprise.

"Yes, you foolish fellow!" said Herr Sesemann and went off to his room to write a letter to the Alm-Uncle.

All this time, Heidi was completely ignorant of what was afoot. Tinette had helped her to dress without uttering a word, for she considered her a common child and not fit to be spoken to.

The letter written, Herr Sesemann returned to the

dining-room where breakfast was ready, and demanded, "Where is the child?"

Heidi was fetched and as she said good morning Herr Sesemann looked into her sad little face. "Now what do you say to this, little one?" he asked kindly.

Heidi looked at him in surprise.

"Don't you know about it yet?" Herr Sesemann laughed. "You are going home to-day."

"Home?" repeated Heidi faintly, turning pale. For a moment she could hardly breathe, she was so overcome by the news.

"Perhaps you don't want to go," suggested Herr Sesemann, smiling.

"Oh, yes, I do want to go home," she replied, her face aglow with pleasure.

"Very well, then, you must take a good breakfast and then off you go in the carriage."

But hard as she tried, Heidi could scarcely swallow a mouthful for excitement. It all seemed like a dream.

"Tell Sebastian to take plenty of provisions for naturally the child can't eat just at present," Herr Sesemann told Fraulein Rottenmeier, who just at that moment entered the room. And turning to Heidi, he said kindly, "Go and join Clara until the carriage arrives."

Heidi rose eagerly and ran upstairs to Clara's room. In the middle of the floor stood a big trunk which Clara had packed with dresses, pinafores, handkerchiefs and all sorts of clothes. "Look what I have packed for you," said Clara. "Aren't you pleased, Heidi? And look, Heidi!" triumphantly she held up a basket. Heidi peeped in and jumped for joy, for inside were twelve beautiful white rolls for the grandmother.

The children were so happily absorbed in their preparations that they had forgotten completely that the time for parting had come, and when the carriage was ready there was no time left for sadness.

Remembering her favourite book, Heidi ran back quickly to her own room and took it from under the pillow, the place where she always kept it, and racing back she put it into the basket with the rolls. Then she went and had a last look in the wardrobe and, sure enough, there was her old red shawl. Heidi wrapped it up and carefully hid it amongst the other luggage so that it would not be seen.

The children had to say good-bye quickly for Herr Sesemann was waiting to see Heidi to the carriage. Fraulein Rottenmeier was waiting at the top of the stairs and somehow a peep of red amongst Heidi's luggage caught her eye. She at once pulled out the red shawl and threw it aside.

"No, Adelheid," she scolded, "you cannot possibly take that old thing with you. Good-bye, then!"

Heidi did not dare lift up the little bundle but looked imploringly at the master of the house with an expression which suggested that her greatest treasure had been taken from her.

"No, no," objected Herr Sesemann very firmly. "The child can take home whatever she pleases, whether it be kittens or tortoises and we won't be upset about it either, Fraulein Rottenmeier."

Heidi quickly lifted up her bundle and her eyes beamed with gratitude. Herr Sesemann shook hands with her, wished her a happy journey and said that he and Clara would always remember her. Heidi thanked him for all his kindness and said finally, "And please say good-bye to the doctor for me and thank him very, very much." She had not forgotten his words of the night before when he had said, "And to-morrow everything will be all right." And now these words had really come true and Heidi was convinced that it was all of his doing.

She was lifted into the carriage, and trunk, basket and provisions followed. Once more Herr Sesemann wished her a good journey and the carriage rolled away.

Very soon Heidi was sitting beside Sebastian in the train, her basket on her lap. For many hours she sat silent. Only now did she fully realise that she was on her way home to the grandfather, the grandmother and Goat Peter, and the familiar scene rose before her eyes. Suddenly she turned anxiously to Sebastian. "Sebastian, are you sure the grandmother on the Alm is not dead?"

"No, no!" he replied comfortingly.

Once more Heidi became preoccupied with her own thoughts, occasionally peeping into the basket. After some time she asked again, "Sebastian, if I only knew for certain that the grandmother is still alive!"

"Yes, yes," said Sebastian, half asleep. "She will be alive. Why should she be dead?"

After a while Heidi fell asleep, too, and slept so soundly that she did not wake up until Sebastian shook her by the arm and said, "Wake up! Wake up! We are in Basle."

The next morning they had to start again on a long train journey and as they reached their destination Heidi was too excited to talk. When she least expected it a voice shouted, "Maienfeld!" Up she jumped from her seat and Sebastian followed. As they stood on the platform beside Heidi's luggage Sebastian looked regretfully after the disappearing train, for he much preferred that comfortable mode of transport to the dangerous climb up into the mountains in this, as he considered it, barbarous country. Cautiously he looked round to see of whom he might inquire the safest road to Dorfli. He spotted a broad-shouldered man loading a cart with big heavy sacks which had just arrived by train. Sebastian addressed his inquiry to him.

"All the roads here are safe," answered the man.

So Sebastian asked which was the best way one could take without being in danger of falling over a precipice, and also how to get a trunk up to Dorfli. The man regarded the trunk and then declared that if it was not too heavy he would take it on his cart as he was on his way there. After further conversation, the man agreed to take both the child and the trunk as far as Dorfli and from there somebody would take her up to the Alm.

"I can go by myself. I know the way from Dorfli to the Alm," said Heidi, who had been listening attentively to the conversation.

Sebastian was greatly relieved not to have to do any climbing. He took Heidi aside and gave her a heavy little leather bag and the letter to the grandfather, explaining; "This little bag is a present from Herr Sesemann. It must go to the bottom of the basket, under the rolls, and you must be very careful with it for Herr Sesemann would be very angry if you were to lose it."

"I won't lose it," said Heidi confidently and at once put both the bag and the letter at the bottom of her basket.

The trunk was hoisted on to the cart and then Sebastian helped Heidi with her basket on to the driver's seat. He shook hands with her and reminded her once more about the contents of the basket. (Sebastian was rather worried as he knew he was supposed to see the child right to her destination.) The driver swung himself up beside Heidi and the cart moved off. Sebastian, glad to have rid himself of a wearisome duty, sat down in the station to wait for the return train.

The man with the cart was the baker from Dorfli who

was taking home his sacks of flour. He had never seen
Heidi before but felt sure this must be the much-discussed
child whose parents he had known. "Aren't you the little
girl who lived with the uncle on the Alm?" he shouted
to Heidi above the noise of the cart.

"Yes," replied Heidi.

"You are soon back, aren't you? Didn't they treat
you well there?"

"No, it wasn't that. Nobody could have been treated
better than I was in Frankfurt."

"What brings you back then?"

"Because Herr Sesemann allowed me."

"But wouldn't you rather have stayed?"

"Oh, I'd rather be with the grandfather on the Alm
than anywhere else in the world!"

"Maybe you'll think differently once you're there,"
muttered the baker. Then he started to whistle and
said no more.

Heidi looked round and trembled with excitement
as she began to recognise the trees on the road and
above, the great towering peaks which seemed to welcome her back like old friends. As they drove into Dorfli
the clock was striking five. A group of women and
children clustered round the cart and wanted to know
where they had come from and where they were going.
As the baker lifted Heidi down she said quickly, "Thank
you. Grandfather will fetch the trunk later," and made to
run off. She was at once stopped by questions from all
sides but she pushed her way through the crowd with
such determination that the people were compelled to
stand aside and let her through.

They were all convinced that she would not go back
to the grandfather if she had anywhere else to go but the
baker quickly enlightened them, declaring that although
she had had the chance to live in a house where she had

everything, it was her own wish to return to the grandfather. This news amazed everybody and it was soon spread around Dorfli that Heidi had given up a luxurious home to return to the hut on the Alm.

As fast as she could, Heidi climbed up from Dorfli. As she reached the top the path got steeper and the basket seemed to get heavier and heavier, so that she was obliged to pause now and then to get her breath. There was only one thought in her mind. Would she find the grandmother still in her usual corner by the spinning wheel? Suddenly she caught sight of the cottage and her heart began to pound. She ran as fast as she could until she reached the door and trembled so much with excitement that she could hardly open it. But at last she was inside and standing in the middle of the little room with no breath left to say a word.

"Dear Lord!" a voice cried from the corner, "that sounded like Heidi. If only I could have her with me again! Who is there?"

"But it *is* Heidi, Grandmother! I am back!" called Heidi and rushed towards the old woman. She put her arms round her and hugged her, unable to speak for joy. At first the grandmother was too surprised to utter a word; then she caressed Heidi's curly head and said, "Yes, it is her hair, and her voice. Thank God that He has granted this to me!" Tears of joy spilled from her blind eyes. "Is it really you, Heidi? Have you come back to me?"

"Yes, Grandmother, it is true," assured Heidi. "Don't cry. I am really back and will come to you every day and never go away again. And you won't have to eat hard bread any more. Look, Grandmother, look!"

Heidi unpacked her basket and piled the twelve rolls in the grandmother's lap.

"Ah, child, what a blessing you bring with you," she said, feeling the rolls, of which there seemed to be a countless number, "but the greatest blessing is you yourself," and again she touched Heidi's hair and her hot cheek. "Speak to me, child," she murmured, "so that I can hear your voice again."

Heidi was in the midst of telling the grandmother how she had feared she might never see her again when the door opened and Peter's mother walked in. For a moment she stood perplexed, then she cried, "Can it possibly be you, Heidi?"

Brigitta's quick glance soon took in Heidi's appearance, and with little gasps of admiration she exclaimed to the grandmother, "Mother, if you could only see what a pretty frock she is wearing and how grand she looks! I hardly recognise her. And this hat with the feather, is it yours, too, Heidi? Put it on and let me see how you look in it."

"No, I don't care about it," replied Heidi. "If you like it, please have it. I still have my old one." Heidi opened the little red bundle and took out her own hat which looked more crushed than ever after the long journey. But that did not trouble Heidi. She still remembered all the grandfather had had to say about hats with feathers, on Dete's last visit. And taking off her pretty frock, she wrapped the red shawl round her shoulders. "But now," she said, taking the grandmother's hand, "I must go home to Grandfather. To-morrow I shall come back. Good night, Grandmother!"

"Yes, come again, Heidi, come again to-morrow," begged the grandmother and pressed the child's hands.

"But why have you taken off your pretty dress?" Brigitta wanted to know.

"Because I would rather go to Grandfather like

this in case he shouldn't recognise me. You hardly knew me at first."

Heidi said good night and went off up to the Alm. The big snowfield at the Scesaplana sparkled in the evening sun. A red shimmer fell on the grass at Heidi's feet and she turned round. She had not remembered, even in her dreams, how beautiful this picture was. The two peaks of the Falknis rose like twin flames, the snowfield was aglow and above it floated rose-tinted clouds. Far below stretched the valley, and above and around everything glittered and sparkled. Tears crept down Heidi's cheeks at the sight of all this splendour. Earnestly she pressed her hands together and thanked God for bringing her home again. She stood still, her heart full of thankfulness, until the light began to fade, and then all at once she ran up the mountain as fast as she could. Presently the tops of the fir trees and then the hut came into view, and there was the grandfather sitting on his bench and smoking his pipe. Heidi ran faster and before the Alm-Uncle was aware of anything Heidi had thrown her basket to the ground and put her two arms round his neck, unable to say more than, "Grandfather! Grandfather! Grandfather!"

The old man could say nothing. For the first time for many years his eyes were wet with tears and he brushed them roughly away with the back of his hand. Then he lifted Heidi on to his knee and looked at her. "So you have come home again, Heidi," he began. "You don't look very much of a lady. Did they send you away?"

"Oh, no, Grandfather. You mustn't think that. They were all very good to me, Clara and Grandmamma and Herr Sesemann. It was just that I couldn't bear being away from you any longer. Sometimes I felt I would choke, but I never said anything because it would have been ungrateful. Then suddenly one morning Herr Sesemann called for me very early—I think maybe it was the doctor who told him—but perhaps it is all in the letter——" and Heidi jumped down and fetched the letter and the little bag from her basket and handed them both to the grandfather.

"I think that belongs to you," he declared, laying the little leather bag beside him on the bench. Then he read the letter and without a word put it into his pocket.

"Do you think you could still drink milk with me?" he asked Heidi and took her hand to go into the hut. "But take your money! You can buy a proper bed with it and enough clothes to last several years."

"I don't need it, Grandfather," assured Heidi. "I have got a bed already and Clara packed such a lot of clothes in my trunk that I shall never have to buy any."

"Take the money and put it into the cupboard, then. Some day you may want it."

Heidi obeyed and followed the grandfather into the hut. Joyfully she ran about and looked into every corner. Then she went up the ladder, but she stopped short whenever she put her head into the loft. "Oh, Grandfather, where is my bed?" she cried reproachfully.

"It will soon be there again," came from below. "How was I to know you were coming back? Come down and drink your milk."

Heidi came down and took her old seat in the high chair. Eagerly she drank her milk as though nothing had ever tasted so delicious. Then she took a deep breath and declared, "There is nothing in the whole world so good as our milk, Grandfather!"

Suddenly a shrill whistle sounded. Quick as lightning Heidi rushed outside, and there were the goats, skipping and jumping down the steep heights with Peter in their midst. Speechlessly he stared at Heidi.

"Good evening, Peter!" she said. "Do you still know me?"

The little goats had evidently recognised her voice, for they rubbed their heads against her eagerly. Heidi was wild with joy to see her old companions once more and called each one by name.

Slowly Peter came towards her. "So you are back again!" he managed to say at last. Then, just as in the old days, he asked, "Will you come up to the pasture, to-morrow?"

"No, not to-morrow, but the next day. To-morrow I must go and see the grandmother."

"I am glad you are back," Peter said, beaming with happiness, and began to urge the goats down the mountain.

When Heidi got back into the cottage her bed was already made up for her. With a sigh of contentment she lay down and slept as she had not done for a whole year. During the night the grandfather got up again and again and listened anxiously to hear if Heidi slept quietly. But Heidi never stirred. Now there was nothing to make her wander about in the night-time for her longing was satisfied. She had seen the mountains again and had heard the wind in the fir trees. She was home on the Alm.

CHAPTER 14

The Bells Ring Out

~~~~~~~~

EIDI STOOD under the fir trees and waited for the Alm-Uncle who was going to take her as far as the grandmother's and then go on to Dorfli to fetch her trunk. She was impatient to hear how the grandmother had enjoyed the white rolls and thought the grandfather would never be finished with his tasks, but at last the old man appeared and announced, to Heidi's satisfaction, "Well, I have finished, so we can go now."

At Goat Peter's cottage they parted and Heidi ran inside. The grandmother heard her step and called lovingly, "Are you there, child? Have you come back again?" She took Heidi's hand and told her how much she had enjoyed the rolls and how much stronger she felt already. Brigitta explained how the grandmother would only take one roll each day for fear they would be finished too soon. At that Heidi exclaimed, "I know what I shall do, Grandmother. I shall write to Clara and I am sure she will send as many rolls as you want."

"That is very good of you," said Brigitta, "but I am afraid they would get very hard and stale. If only I had money! The baker in Dorfli makes them too, but I can't afford to buy them. I have hardly enough money for the ordinary black bread."

"Oh, but I have lots of money!" the child cried delightedly. "Now I know how I shall spend it. Every day Grandmother will have a white roll and two on Sundays and Peter will get them in Dorfli."

"No, no, my child," remonstrated the grandmother. "The money you have got is not for that; you must give it to the grandfather and he will tell you what to do with it."

But Heidi took no notice and continued to chatter happily, "Now Grandmother can eat a roll every day and will get quite strong. Perhaps it's only dark for you because you are so weak, Grandmother."

The grandmother said nothing. She did not want to spoil the child's joy.

Suddenly Heidi caught sight of the grandmother's hymn book and a new thought struck her :

"Grandmother, I can read now. Shall I read to you one of the hymns from your old book?"

"Yes, indeed," replied the grandmother, both surprised and delighted. "But do you really know how to read, child?"

Heidi had climbed on a chair and lifted down the dusty book which had lain untouched on the shelf for a very long time.

She blew the dust off and then sat down on the stool beside the old woman, asking which hymn she wanted to hear.

"Whichever you like, child! Whichever you like!" And she waited in eager expectation while Heidi turned over the pages and read softly a line here and there.

"Here is one about the sun. I shall read that one, Grandmother."

And Heidi read the hymn aloud, very touchingly.

The grandmother sat with folded hands while Heidi read and the face of the aged woman shone with an indescribable joy such as Heidi had never seen before, and her eyes glistened with tears. When the child stopped reading, "Once more, Heidi, please. Read it once more," she begged, and Heidi read the hymn again.

"Oh, Heidi, that is enough to fill my heart with light. How comforting the words are!"

As the grandmother spoke, there was a knock at the window and the grandfather stood outside, beckoning Heidi to come home. She went at once, but not without promising the grandmother that she would come again to-morrow. She was completely happy because she could make the grandmother's life cheerful again. It was an even greater source of happiness to her than the goats and the pasture.

Heidi had so much to tell the grandfather, particularly about the rolls. "Surely, Grandfather," she said, "if Grandmother won't take the money you will give me money from the bag so that I can give it to Peter to buy the rolls every day!"

"What about a bed, Heidi?" asked the grandfather. "A proper bed for you would be nice and there would still be plenty left over for the rolls?"

But Heidi gave him no peace and at last the old man said, "The money is yours to do with as you please. You will be able to buy rolls for the Grandmother with it for many, many years."

Heidi was jubilant. "Oh, Grandfather, isn't everything wonderful!" Then she became serious. "If God had answered when I prayed to come here at once, everything would have been different. I would only have come for a short time and Grandmother would only have got a few rolls and I wouldn't have been able to read to her. But God has thought it out much better than I ever could, just as Grandmamma told me in Frankfurt. Everything has turned out as she said. Oh, how glad I am that God did not let me have my way! Now I shall always pray as Grandmamma taught me and if God does not do what I ask I shall think at once, 'I am sure it is just the same as at Frankfurt and God knows a much better way.' So we will pray every day, please, Grandfather, and we will never forget Him so that He does not forget us."

"And if somebody does forget Him?" murmured the grandfather.

"Oh, it will be the worse for him! Because then God will forget *him*, and nobody will pity him because he ran away from God who could have helped him."

"That is true, Heidi. But how do you know?"

"From Grandmamma. She explained it all to me."

The grandfather walked on silently, then, lost in his own thoughts, he said, "But nobody can go back once he has forgotten God and God has forgotten him for ever."

"Oh, no, Grandfather! It's possible to go back. I know that, too, from Grandmamma, and it even says so in the lovely story in my book, but you have not read it yet. As soon as we are home you shall hear what a beautiful story it is."

As soon as they reached the top of the hill Heidi ran into the cottage to get her book and returned presently with it under her arm. The grandfather, busy with his own thoughts, was seated on the bench. Heidi climbed up beside him and opened her book at her favourite story.

Now Heidi began to read the story of the Prodigal Son who, although he had all he could wish for at home tending his father's flock, asked for his share of his father's wealth so that he could go out into the world and be his own master. After he had foolishly spent all he had, he was obliged to work as a swine-herd with nothing to wear but rags and nothing to eat but the husks which the pigs left. Then he remembered his father and thought what an ungrateful son he had been, and he wept bitterly. So he decided, 'I shall go to my father and ask forgiveness and say to him, "I am not worthy to be called thy son, make me one of thy day-labourers." ' But when he was still a great distance from his father's house, his father recognised him and hastened forward——

"And what do you think happens now, Grandfather?" Heidi could not help stopping to ask. "Do you think the father is still angry and will say to him, ' Go away! ' Listen now to what happens next! "

"And when the father saw him coming he had compassion on him and embraced him, and the son said, ' Father, I have sinned against Heaven and in thy sight and am not worthy to be called thy son.' But his father said to his servants, ' Bring the best robe for him. Put a ring on his finger and bring shoes for his feet. And bring forth the fatted calf and kill it and let us eat and be merry, for this, my son, was dead and is alive again; he was lost and is found.'

"Isn't that a beautiful story, Grandfather?" asked Heidi when she saw that he was still absorbed in his thoughts.

"Yes, Heidi, the story is beautiful," answered the grandfather, his face still grave. So Heidi was silent for a while and looked at the pictures in her book.

A few hours later when Heidi had been asleep for a long time, the grandfather climbed up the ladder and put his lamp beside her bed so that its light fell on the sleeping child. She was lying with folded hands, as if she had fallen asleep saying her prayers. On her little face was an expression of peace and trust. For a long time the old man stood gazing at the child, then he folded his hands and half aloud he prayed with bent head, "Father, I have sinned against Heaven and in Thy sight and am not worthy to be called Thy son." As he spoke tears rolled down the old man's cheeks.

Early next morning the Alm-Uncle stood in front of his hut, smiling gently as he looked around him. It was a beautiful Sunday morning and he could hear the church bells ringing down in the valley. He went back into the hut and called up to the loft, "Get up, Heidi! The sun has risen. Put on your nice frock for we are going to church together this morning."

Heidi was soon dressed in her pretty Frankfurt clothes and came downstairs quickly, her curiosity aroused by this unusual summons from the Alm-Uncle; but great was her surprise when she caught a glimpse of him. "Oh, Grandfather, I have never seen you in this coat with the silver buttons. How nice you look in your Sunday coat!"

The old man smiled and said, "You too, in your pretty dress. Come along now!" He took Heidi's hand in his and they walked down the mountain together. The bells were ringing on every side and the sound of them filled the whole valley and rose up echoing among the mountains. As they descended, the peels sounded louder and richer and Heidi listened rapturously. "Listen, Grandfather! It is like a great festival."

When the grandfather and Heidi entered the church the singing had already begun so they sat down together at the back. But before the hymn was finished there was subdued whispering on all sides, "The Alm-Uncle! Did you see the Alm-Uncle?"

Soon everybody knew that the Alm-Uncle was in church and the women, hardly able to believe, kept turning their heads to look. When the sermon began, everybody became more attentive and forgot, for the time being, about the uncle.

As soon as the service was finished the old uncle walked with the child in the direction of the pastor's house. Some of the people followed him curiously and when they saw him and the child go inside, they gathered in excited groups to discuss the extraordinary event, for they could not imagine what had brought the old man down from his mountaintop. It soon became evident that many of them were beginning to change their opinion of the old man. They had noticed what great care he took of the little one and surely, they thought, he cannot be so very wicked or he would be afraid to face the pastor. Then the baker reminded them, "Didn't I tell you! What child would give up a wonderful home with the best life can offer to go back to a grandfather who had been unkind and of whom she is afraid?" And so a friendly feeling for the grandfather began to spread amongst the people and they waited patiently at the pastor's door as though to welcome back an old friend who had been gone a long time.

The uncle knocked at the door of the pastor's study and the pastor greeted him as though he had expected the old man. His appearance in church had not escaped the pastor's notice and he shook hands warmly. At first the Alm-Uncle could not find words, then, pulling himself together, he began, "Pastor, I have come to ask you to forget the words I spoke to you on the Alm and not to hold it against me that I was too obstinate to take your well-meant advice. I see now that you were right and I was wrong, so I am following your advice and I would like to take the house in Dörfli for the winter, for the cold season up there is not good for the child. She is too delicate. Of course, the people here do not trust me and I deserve no better."

The kind eyes of the pastor brightened with joy. Once more he grasped the old man's hand and said with deep emotion, "Neighbour, I am sincerely glad; and you will never have cause to regret coming back to live amongst us. You will always be welcome in my house and I hope to spend many a pleasant winter evening with you for I value your friendship. And we shall also find playmates for the little one."

The pastor laid his hand affectionately on Heidi's curly head, and taking her by the hand, accompanied them both to the door. When they stood outside on the doorstep he bid them good-bye and everybody noticed that the pastor shook hands with the Alm-Uncle as if they were the best of friends.

As soon as the door closed the old man was assailed by friendly greetings from every one, "How nice to see you again, Uncle!" "It's good to see you back, Uncle. I have been wanting to have a talk with you for a long time." And when the Uncle told them that he was going to live again in his old house in Dorfli for the winter months, there was such a chorus of joyful shouts that it seemed as though the Alm-Uncle were the most popular person in Dorfli. The farming people accompanied the old man and the child far up the mountain path and when they said farewell every one invited him to call next time he was down. When they parted, the old man followed them with his eyes and his face reflected an inner light so that Heidi could not take her eyes off him. "Grandfather," she said, "to-day you look nicer and nicer every minute. I have never seen you like this before."

"Do you think so?" asked the old man, smiling. "You see, Heidi, I am so happy to-day. To be at peace with God and man is good! God was good to me when He sent you to the Alm."

When they arrived at Goat Peter's hut, the grandfather opened the door and they walked inside.

"Good morning, Grandmother!" he said. "I think we will have to do some more patching before the autumn winds come."

"Mercy!" exclaimed the grandmother. "That is the uncle!" and her voice was both surprised and pleased. "Now I can thank you for all you have done for us, Uncle. God bless you! God bless you!" And when he held her trembling hand she said, "If I have ever hurt you, don't punish me by taking Heidi away from me. Oh, you do not know what the child means to me." And she held Heidi close to her.

"Have no fear, Grandmother. I shall not punish either you or myself. We shall stay together now and, if God wills it, for a long time."

Now Peter rushed in noisily and evidently in a great hurry. He held a letter in his hand which was a rare enough occurrence to account for his excitement. It was a letter for Heidi which had been given to Peter at the post office in Dorfli. Heidi opened her letter and read it aloud. It was from Clara.

She told Heidi how dull it had been since she had gone and how, for this reason, she had persuaded her father to take her to Ragatz next autumn so that she might have a chance of seeing her again. Grandmamma wished to come too, for she also wished to visit Heidi and the grandfather on the Alm; and Grandmamma was sending some coffee so that the grandmother would not have to eat the rolls dry. And she was looking forward to visiting the grandmother herself.

There were so many questions to ask and so much to discuss after this news that even the grandfather did not notice how quickly time was passing. Everybody was happy about the news but, as the grandmother said, the greatest delight of all was to see an old friend return like old times. "Come again, soon, Uncle, and you, child, to-morrow!"

They both promised. But now it was time to leave. As in the morning the bells had greeted them, so now the

122

peaceful evening chimes accompanied them on their way up to the sunny Alm cottage which shone with an air of Sunday calm in the red glow of the evening sky.

CHAPTER 15

Preparations for a Journey

∿∿∿∿∿∿

IT WAS A sunny morning in September and the good doctor, who had been the cause of Heidi's going home, was on his way to the Sesemanns' house. There was a look of great sadness on his face and he seemed to have aged considerably since the spring. The doctor had had an only daughter in whom, since the death of his wife, he had found his only happiness. A few months before, she had died and, ever since, all the doctor's brightness and cheerfulness had gone.

Sebastian opened the door with marked civility, for the doctor was not only the best friend of the master but also of his little daughter, and because of his warmth and kindness was beloved by every one in the house.

"Everything all right?" he asked Sebastian in his pleasant voice as he preceded the servant upstairs.

"Ah, I am glad you are here!" exclaimed Herr Sesemann as he stepped forward to welcome his friend. "We must definitely re-discuss this Swiss journey. Do you still stick by your decision in spite of the fact that Clara's health shows signs of improvement?"

"My dear Sesemann, what am I to think of you!" replied the doctor. "This is the third time to-day you have called me in to ask the same question."

"Yes, you are perfectly right and I cannot blame you for becoming impatient; but you must understand, my dear friend, how difficult it is for me to deny the child now, at the last minute, something which I promised her so faithfully and to which she has been looking forward for months. It is only the prospect of this journey and the thought of seeing her friend again which has enabled Clara to suffer so patiently these last bad weeks and now, suddenly, I am to deprive the poor child of this joy. I simply cannot do it."

"Sesemann, it has to be done," replied the doctor firmly, and when he saw his friend silent and depressed he continued, "Now think it out for yourself. For years Clara hasn't had such a bad summer as this last one. There can be no question of travelling without risk of the worst consequences. And after all, it is September, and although there is a chance that it is still fine up there it may very easily be cold. The days are getting shorter and the journey from Ragatz to the Alm would take several hours as Clara would have to be carried up the mountain. In short, Sesemann, it is quite impossible. But I shall speak to her myself. She is a sensible child. If she is taken to Ragatz next May for very special care and if she is stronger she will enjoy the excursion up the mountain far more than now. Only with the greatest care and attention can she have a chance of recovery."

Herr Sesemann rose and walked up and down the room as was his habit when something occupied his mind. Suddenly he tapped his friend on the shoulder. "Doctor, I have a suggestion to make. You don't look well and are not the same as you used to be. You need a change and do you know what has occurred to me? You should go and visit Heidi on the Alm in our name."

This suggestion surprised the doctor very much and he started to make objections, but Herr Sesemann gave him no opportunity. He was so enthusiastic about his new plan that he took his friend by the arm and drew him into Clara's room.

Herr Sesemann took Clara's hand in his and began to talk about the Swiss journey and how he himself had looked forward to it. He passed quickly over the main point—that it was impossible now for Clara to go—and then told her of his latest plan to persuade their good friend, the doctor, to take this holiday.

Tears came into Clara's eyes although she tried to hide them for her father's sake, but it was a great disappointment to her to have to give up this journey which had been her only joy and comfort during many lonely hours. She knew, however, that her father would only deny her something which would do her harm; so she swallowed her tears and turned her thoughts to the only remaining hope. She took the doctor's hand and said imploringly :

"Please, doctor, go and see Heidi and then come back and tell me what it is like there and how Heidi is getting on; and the grandfather, and Peter and the goats. I feel I know them all so well! And then you can take to Heidi all the things I have for her, and something for the grandmother. Please go, doctor, and I'll take as much cod liver oil as you like."

It may not have been this promise which altogether decided the doctor but he certainly replied smilingly:

"Then I suppose I must go, Clara, if we are to see you grow plump and strong! And when have you decided I am to start?"

"As soon as possible, doctor. To-morrow morning," replied Clara.

"She is quite right," interrupted her father. "The weather is fine and it would be a pity to miss a single day which you could enjoy on the Alm."

The doctor could not help laughing a little. "Soon you'll reproach me for not being there already, Sesemann. I see I shall have to make haste."

But Clara still detained him. She had to give him lots of messages for Heidi. The doctor promised to deliver them all faithfully and to bring back a full account of everything that happened.

The servants of a household have a strange capacity for knowing what is going on long before they are informed about it by the master. Sebastian, as he opened the front door for the doctor, said with his usual deference: "May I ask the doctor to give my regards to the little fraulein?"

"Ah, Sebastian," the doctor smiled, "you know already about my going?"

Sebastian looked embarrassed, "Well, I—not exactly —as a matter of fact—— well, you see, I just happened to go into the dining-room when I heard the little fraulein's name mentioned, and then I thought——"

"I see! I see!" smiled the doctor. "Good-bye, Sebastian! I'll be sure to remember your message."

The doctor stepped across the threshold, and then jumped back again quickly. The doorway was blocked by Fraulein Rottenmeier returning from her walk. It was a very gusty day and the wind blew out her skirts so that she looked like a ship in full sail. The wind was so strong she was blown right into the doorway and, gasping for breath, crashed into the doctor. The poor lady was very much upset by this loss of dignity for she had a great admiration for the doctor, but he very quickly smoothed her down and told her of his plans, asking her in a most amiable voice to pack the parcel for Heidi in the way in which only she could do it. Then off he went.

Clara had expected that Fraulein Rottenmeier would make all sorts of objections to sending the many presents to Heidi, but she was mistaken. Fraulein Rottenmeier was in an exceptionally good temper and Clara was allowed to watch everything being packed. This was not an easy task, for the presents were all of different shapes and sizes. There was the little warm coat with the hood for Heidi; then a thick warm shawl for the grandmother and also a large cake as a change from the rolls. Then there was a delicious sausage which Clara had at first meant for Peter but had later decided to send to Brigitta, since there might be a danger of Peter eating it all himself, and Brigitta could be depended upon to divide it up for supper. There was a packet of tobacco for the grandfather who was so fond of his pipe, and last of all, there were a lot of mysterious little packages which Clara made up specially to be put in as surprises for Heidi.

At last the job was done and an imposing-looking parcel lay on the floor ready for transport. Clara gazed at it blissfully, imagining Heidi's squeals of delight when it arrived.

Fraulein Rottenmeier rang for Sebastian and with an energetic swing he lifted the parcel on to his shoulder and carried it off to be despatched at once to the doctor's house.

CHAPTER 16

A Visitor to the Alm

~~~~~~~~

THE MORNING SKY was all aglow, shedding its light upon the mountains, and a fresh breeze stirred in the fir trees, swaying their ancient branches. Heidi opened her eyes, awakened by the sound of the wind in the trees, and jumping out of bed, dressed herself very quickly. When she came down the ladder, the grandfather was already standing outside and was looking at the sky to see what sort of weather it was going to be. Little pink clouds floated across the sky and gradually more and more blue patches appeared. The sun was just rising and touched the mountain tops with gold.

"Oh, how lovely!" cried Heidi. Then, "Good morning, Grandfather!"

"Are you awake already?" he said, patting the child's head.

The grandfather went off to milk the goats and brought them out ready for their climb up to the pastures. There came the sound of Peter's whistle and presently Heidi was surrounded by the whole flock. Peter whistled again, shrilly, and the goats moved off.

"Are you coming with us to-day?" he asked.

"No, Peter, I can't come to-day," replied Heidi. "The friends from Frankfurt may arrive at any moment and I must be here when they come."

"That's what you always say," grumbled Peter. "Anyway, the uncle is always here."

Just at that point the uncle himself called out, "What's

wrong with the army to-day, it isn't on the move? Is it the General's fault or is it the troops'?"

Peter turned at once and cracked his whip in the air, and the goats, who knew the sound well, started off up the mountain with Peter trotting after them.

Since Heidi had come back she thought of all sorts of things to do about the house which had not occurred to her before. Every morning she made her bed carefully, then she went downstairs and tidied the kitchen. She put the chairs straight and anything which was lying about she put into the cupboard. Next she would get out a duster, and climbing on to a chair, would rub the table until it shone. All this pleased the grandfather and he would look round, saying, "The house is so well kept nowadays it always looks as though it were Sunday! Heidi's trip certainly hasn't been in vain!"

To-day Heidi had begun her chores as usual but the beautiful weather seemed to draw her outside. A sunbeam slanting through the open window seemed to be calling: "Come Heidi! Come out!" She simply could not stay indoors any longer and ran outside. The sunlight sparkled on the mountains and shone down on the valley. Heidi had to sit down for a minute and look about her. The grandfather was working in the shed and came out from time to time to look smilingly at the child. He had just gone back to his work when Heidi called out loudly, "Grandfather! Grandfather! Come quickly!" The old man came out at once, afraid that something had happened to the child. He saw Heidi running towards the path, calling as she went, "They are coming! They are coming! The doctor is first!"

Heidi rushed forward to welcome her old friend who stretched out his hand in greeting. As soon as she reached him she clasped his outstretched arm affectionately. "Good morning, doctor! I am so grateful to you."

"God bless you, Heidi! And what is it you are grateful to me for?"

"For arranging it so that I could come home," explained the child.

The doctor's face brightened with joy. He had not expected such a welcome. He had climbed the steep mountain path feeling lonely and depressed and with never a thought for the beautiful scenery around him. Convinced that Heidi would hardly even recognise him again he had pictured the disappointment his arrival without the expected friends would cause. But instead, here was Heidi beaming with joy and full of love and gratitude, and still clinging to his arm.

With fatherly tenderness the doctor took the child by the hand. "Come, Heidi. Take me to your grandfather and show me where you live."

But Heidi did not go on. Her gaze was fixed on the path down the mountain and her little face showed disappointment. "Where are Clara and Grandmamma?" she asked.

"I have something to tell you, Heidi, and I know you will be as sorry about it as I am," replied the doctor. "You see, Heidi, I have come alone. Clara has been very ill and could not travel, so the grandmamma did not come either, But in the spring, when the days begin to get warmer and longer, they will certainly come."

Heidi looked perplexed. It was difficult for her to realise that everything she had looked forward to was not to be. The doctor stood silently before her and there was no sound save the sighing of the wind in the fir trees. Then it occurred to Heidi that after all the doctor had come and she looked up at him. The eyes that looked down into hers were sad. Heidi had never seen him look like this in Frankfurt and her heart was at once full of sorrow for him. No doubt, she decided, it was because

Clara and the grandmamma could not come and she tried to think quickly of a way in which to comfort him.

"Oh, it won't be long until the spring and then they'll be sure to come, won't they?" she asked. "The winter is never very long here and when they do come they will be able to stay much longer. Clara will certainly like that! Now let's go up to the grandfather."

Hand in hand with the doctor, she climbed up to the cottage and called out cheerfully to the grandfather. "They haven't come yet, but it won't be long."

The doctor was no stranger to the grandfather, for Heidi had talked about him a great deal. The old man welcomed his guest heartily and then the two men sat down on the bench before the cottage and there was still a little place for Heidi beside the doctor. The doctor started to explain :

"Herr Sesemann wanted me to come and I allowed myself to be persuaded because I have not been well for quite a time and I thought the fresh mountain air would do me good. Heidi," said the doctor, stooping towards her, "there will be something coming up here which has travelled with me all the way from Frankfurt—something which will give you more pleasure than the old doctor."

Heidi was intensely interested to know what it could be but the doctor would not give a hint.

The grandfather encouraged the doctor to spend the beautiful autumn days on the Alm, or at least, to come up every fine day. "I cannot invite you to stay here, as I have no accommodation, but if you would take a room down in Dörfli in the pleasant little inn instead of going back to Ragatz you could come up here in the mornings. There are many places round about which I would take pleasure in showing you."

This proposal delighted the doctor and so it was settled.

Time had passed quickly and it was now noon. The Alm-Uncle rose and went into the cottage and brought back a little table which he placed in front of the bench. "Now, Heidi. Fetch everything we need for the meal," he ordered. " The doctor has to be content with our simple fare but he must admit that the dining-room is very pleasant."

"It is, indeed," agreed the doctor, looking down into the sunlit valley. "I gladly accept your kind invitation. Everything is bound to taste good in such surroundings."

Heidi ran to and fro like a busy little squirrel and brought whatever she could find in the cupboard. The grandfather prepared the meal and appeared presently with the steaming milk jug and golden-brown toasted cheese. From the meat which he had cured himself he cut nice thin slices and the doctor ate more heartily than he had done for a whole year.

"Yes, Clara must certainly come here," he said. "It will give her new strength, and if her appetite is as good as mine has been to-day she'll grow plump and strong in no time."

As the doctor spoke, a man appeared coming up the path with a big bundle on his back. Panting, he arrived at the hut and put it down with a sigh of relief. "This is the thing which has come with me all the way from Frankfurt," said the doctor, rising. The bundle was opened and when the first wrapping had been taken off he said: "Now, child, you go on and get out the treasure for yourself."

Heidi looked with big, astonished eyes at each item as it was unwrapped. The doctor lifted the lid of one of the boxes. "Look, Heidi. Something the grandmother can have with her coffee!"

Heidi picked up the cake and skipped around with it joyfully: "Oh, a cake for the grandmother!" Heidi wanted to go down at once to the grandmother with the presents, but the grandfather persuaded her to wait until the evening when she could accompany the doctor on his way down and take the presents at the same time.

Now Heidi found the packet of tobacco and handed it to the grandfather who started at once to fill his pipe. The two men went back and sat down on the bench, leaving Heidi to continue her inspection of Clara's parcel alone. After she had admired them all sufficiently, Heidi put away the many presents and came back to where the men were sitting. As soon as there was a gap in the conversation she addressed their guest very solemnly:

"Nothing has given me so much pleasure as your visit, doctor."

The two men could not help laughing at her childish gravity.

As the sun set behind the mountains, the guest rose to take his leave and begin his walk down to Dorfli. The grandfather took the presents under his arm, the box with the cake, the big sausage and the shawl; the doctor took Heidi's hand and so all three walked down to Goat Peter's cottage. Here Heidi said good night to the doctor and asked: "Would you like to come with the goats to-morrow?"

"Very well, Heidi. We'll go together," he replied. Now the two men walked on down the valley and Heidi entered the cottage; taking first the cake box, then bringing in the big sausage, and last of all the shawl. She brought everything very close to the grandmother so that the old woman would be able to touch the presents; but she laid the shawl on her knees.

"It has all come from Clara and the grandmamma in

Frankfurt," she told the astonished Brigitta and the grandmother.

"Aren't you delighted with the cake, Grandmother?" Heidi wanted to know.

"Yes, Heidi. What kind people they must be!" Then she felt the warm, soft shawl and said, "How cosy it will be in the winter-time! I never dreamt I would possess anything so luxurious."

Heidi was surprised that the grandmother was more pleased about the shawl than the cake.

Brigitta was gazing at the sausage with a look in her eyes little short of worship. Never in her life had she seen such an enormous sausage.

Then Peter came rushing in. "The Alm-Uncle is just behind me, Heidi——" Peter stopped and gasped with astonishment as he caught sight of the sausage.

Although the grandfather never passed the cottage without stopping to say a few cheerful words to the grandmother, to-day it was too late for Heidi, so he only called good night through the door as Heidi ran out to join him. He took her hand and under the star-lit sky the two climbed up to their peaceful mountain hut.

CHAPTER 17

A Compensation

❧❧❧❧❧

ARLY NEXT MORNING the doctor climbed up to the Alm with Peter and the goats. The man and the boy walked in silence. In vain the doctor had tried to start up a conversation with the boy but Peter remained obstinately silent. Up at the Alm cottage Heidi waited with her two goats.

"Are you coming?" asked Peter as he did every morning.

"Of course, if the doctor is coming, too," replied Heidi.

Peter cast a suspicious glance at the gentleman.

The Alm-Uncle came out of the hut carrying the lunch bag which he slung across Peter's shoulder. It was heavier than usual, for the uncle had put in something extra for the doctor in case he decided to stay long enough on the pasture to have his lunch with the children. When Peter felt the extra weight a grin spread across his face and the sulky look vanished. His thoughts were busy with the special tit-bits which the uncle might have put in the bag.

Now the trip started. The doctor took Heidi's hand. He had no difficulty this time in making conversation, for Heidi had so much to say about the goats, the mountains, the flowers and the birds, that time passed quickly and they soon found themselves at the pasture. Heidi led the doctor to her favourite spot where she liked to sit, and the doctor sat down on the grass beside her, casting a contented glance around him at the wide, green,

135

sunlit valley. Heidi's eyes sparkled with happiness and she glanced round at her friend to see if he too was enchanted with the beautiful scenery. The doctor had been sitting, silent and thoughtful, but when he met Heidi's eager, inquiring eyes, he said, "Yes, Heidi, it is beautiful, but if one's heart is sad how is it possible to enjoy all this beauty? Can you tell me?"

"Oh!" Heidi exclaimed confidently. "No one is ever sad here. That only happens in Frankfurt."

The doctor smiled quietly, then he asked again, "But if somebody brings all the sadness from Frankfurt up here, Heidi, do you know what to do then?"

"When we don't know what to do we have only to tell God about our troubles," said Heidi seriously.

"Well, my dear, that seems to be a good idea," remarked the doctor, "but what if God Himself has sent the sorrow? What can one say to Him, then?"

Heidi had to think about this. "Then, we must wait," she said, "and just keep thinking, 'soon God will make things right.' We have only to have a little patience and not run away; then something will turn up and we will see quite clearly that all the time it was all for the best. At the time we only think of the sadness and cannot imagine things will ever be right again."

"You have a wonderful faith, Heidi, and you must never lose it." The doctor was silent, gazing at the towering mountains above them. Then he said again, "You see, Heidi, when someone has a great grief he cannot enjoy anything lovely, and beauty, like this around us, only makes him more sad. Can you understand that?"

Heidi thought sadly of the old grandmother who would never see again the splendour of the sun and the mountains and for a while she said nothing. Then, "Yes, I can understand that," she said softly. "That's how it was with the grandmother until I read the hymns for her from the old book. She says they made everything light for her again and made her happy."

"Can you remember any of the hymns, Heidi?" asked the doctor.

"Yes, shall I say one to you?" replied Heidi eagerly.

The doctor nodded, and Heidi folded her hands and started to recite the grandmother's favourite hymn.

All this time Peter had been standing apart and growing more and more angry because the old gentleman sat beside Heidi all the time so that Peter had not once had a chance to speak to her. He felt so cross, he stood behind the doctor and shook his fist at him. Peter knew by the sun that it was midday and time for lunch, so he called out at the top of his voice, "Dinnertime!"

Heidi got up to bring the rucksack to where they sat, but the doctor said he was not hungry and only wanted a glass of milk. Heidi did not feel very hungry either, so she ran to Peter and asked him to fetch two bowls of milk, one for the doctor and one for herself. Peter looked at her in surprise and asked, "What about all the food in the rucksack?"

"You can have it, Peter," replied Heidi, "but bring the milk first."

Peter had never been so quick in all his life and when he opened the rucksack and saw all the good food he was ashamed of making such faces at the doctor's back. Now he cast a silent apology in the doctor's direction and proceeded to enjoy a very hearty meal.

Heidi and the doctor wandered about together and talked for a long time until the doctor decided it was time for him to go home. Heidi accompanied him down the mountain as far as the Alm hut and then he went on alone, turning now and again to see Heidi still standing on the same spot and waving to him just as his own little daughter might have done.

The doctor came up to the Alm every morning and sometimes went out with the Alm-Uncle whose conversation he enjoyed very much, for the old man knew the ways of all the wild animals and had many interesting stories to tell.

And so the lovely month of September passed. One morning the doctor did not look quite so happy as usual and told them that this would be his last day and that he would have to return to Frankfurt. "I am very sad to go," he admitted, "for I feel now as if the Alm were my home."

The Alm-Uncle was sorry to hear this news of the doctor's departure for he too had enjoyed his companionship. Heidi could hardly believe that her dear friend had to go and she looked at him beseechingly, but the doctor's smile told her that his visit was at an end. She accompanied him a little of the way until the doctor stopped and said lovingly, stroking her curly hair, "Heidi, I have to go away now. How I would love to take you with me to Frankfurt!"

Heidi recalled Frankfurt, with its many houses and long streets. She remembered Fraulein Rottenmeier and Tinette and replied despondently, "I would rather you came back to us."

"You are right. That will be better," said the doctor. "Good-bye, then, Heidi." His kind eyes looked down on her for an instant and then he turned away quickly and continued his walk down to the valley.

Heidi did not move. The sight of tears in the doctors eyes had upset her and suddenly she started to cry. Then she ran after the doctor as fast as she could, and as soon as she was beside him she sobbed, "I want to come with you! Just let me go back and tell Grandfather!"

The doctor tried to soothe the excited child. "Oh, my dear Heidi," he comforted her, "you must stay here among the fir trees or you may become ill again. But you can promise me this: If I should ever become ill and lonely would you come then and stay with me?"

"Oh, yes, I would come at once. I love you nearly as much as the grandfather."

Once again the doctor said farewell and Heidi stood and waved as long as he remained in sight. As he turned for the last time he whispered to himself, "It is good to live up there. One is restored, body and soul, and knows again what it is to be happy."

CHAPTER 18

Winter in Dorfli

~~~~~~~~

SNOW LAY HIGH around the Alm cottage until the windows appeared to be level with the ground. If the Alm-Uncle had still been living there he would have to have done the same as Peter did every day. When snow had fallen during the night Peter had to jump out of the window, and if there was no frost he sank so deeply into the snow that he had to struggle with both hands and feet to get out again. Then his mother would hand him a shovel and he would scrape a path to the door. But if there was severe frost the house was shut in altogether except for a little window through which only Peter was able to creep. But the great advantage of the frost was that once Peter got through the little window he would be on hard, frozen snow. His mother would hand him his little sleigh through the window and Peter could go where he pleased, for the whole Alm was one huge sledging track.

The Alm-Uncle had kept his word. As soon as the first snows began to fall he had shut up the cottage and the shed and had taken Heidi and the goats down to Dorfli to live. Near the church stood a building which had, once upon a time, been a mansion house. Although it was now half in ruins it still retained something of its former dignity. When the uncle had come to Dorfli with his son, Tobias, he had lived in this neglected house, and since that time it had been empty, for no one could live in it who did not know how to close up all the gaps and holes to keep out the wind which blew out the candles and made draughts all through the dilapidated old house.

But all this the uncle could fix, and when he had decided to spend the winter in Dorfli he had come down many times in the autumn to repair the house. Then, in October, he and Heidi had taken up their abode.

Entering from the back, one came first into a tumble-down building where, on one side, the wall had collapsed completely. Although the other wall was half in ruins the arch of an old window was still visible but thickly overgrown with ivy. The roof was vaulted and this had apparently been the chapel.

Next one entered a large hall where the walls and the ceiling had partly collapsed, and to prevent further ruin, strong pillars had been put in for support. Here the Alm-Uncle had built a partition and had covered the ground with straw for this was to be the goat-house.

After going through many passages where in places the broken roof revealed patches of sky, one at last entered, through a heavy oak door, a spacious room which was still in good condition. The four strong walls with dark panelling were unbroken, and in one corner a stove reached nearly to the ceiling. On its white tiles big blue pictures were painted, representing old castles buried amidst high trees, huntsmen with their dogs or quiet lakes bordered by shady trees with a fisher-man in the foreground. A bench was built all round the stove and here one could sit and study the pictures.

This attracted Heidi at once, and as soon as they entered the room she ran to the stove, sat down on the bench and began to look at the pictures. But as she slid along and round towards the back of the stove she found some-thing else to attract her attention. Between stove and wall four boards had been put up. It might have been a place for storing apples but there were no apples there now and it was, quite obviously, going to be Heidi's bed just like the one on the Alm; a high straw bed with a sheet on it and the sack as a cover. Heidi was overjoyed. "Oh, Grandfather! This is going to be my room. How nice! But where are you going to sleep?"

"Your room has to be near the stove to keep you warm," declared the grandfather. "But you shall see mine, too."

Heidi ran through the huge room behind the grandfather who opened a door on the other side. This led into a small room where the old man had made up his bed. Then there was another door, and Heidi stood amazed when she looked into the spacious kitchen. In this room there were many signs of the grandfather's activity but there still remained a great deal of work to be done to fill up all the holes and crannies through which the wind still whistled.

Heidi was delighted with their new home, and the next day when Peter came she showed him all over the house, for she had already explored every corner.

Four days after they had settled down Heidi announced to the grandfather one morning that she must go and visit the grandmother. "I can't leave her alone any longer," she said. But the grandfather would not agree.

"Not to-day or to-morrow," he said. "The Alm is covered fathom-deep in snow, and it is still falling; Peter can hardly get through. A little one like you would soon be buried and no one would be able to find you. Wait a little until it freezes and then you can walk up quite comfortably."

At first Heidi was impatient at the thought of having to wait, but the days were busy and passed quickly. Every morning and afternoon she went to school and learned eagerly. She hardly ever saw Peter there for he seldom turned up. The teacher was a kind man and would remark tolerantly, "Peter absent to-day again! Ah, well, the snow is lying high, he won't be able to get through."

But in the evening, when school was finished, Peter always seemed able to come down to see Heidi!

One morning, when Peter, as usual, sprang from the window into the snow he found that it had hardened with the strong frost of the previous night. The hard ice came as a surprise to him and he could not stop himself sliding off down the Alm which was frozen over as hard as iron. This delighted Peter because he knew that Heidi would be able to come up now to the cottage. Quickly he rushed back to the house and hurriedly swallowing his breakfast he announced, "I must be off to school!"

"Yes, go and learn as much as you can," said his mother.

Peter climbed through the little window, got on to his sledge and went shooting rapidly down the mountain. He went so fast that when he reached Dorfli he was quite unable to stop and the sledge skimmed along until it reached level ground when it stopped of its own accord. Peter got up and looked about. The headlong drive had taken him almost to Maienfeld. It would take him an hour to climb up again and that would be much too late for school thought Peter, so he might as well take his time. He arrived back in Dorfli just as Heidi and the grandfather were sitting down to dinner. Peter entered and as he had something special to tell them to-day he began right away.

"It's done it!" he fairly shouted.

"Eh! What has?" asked the old man. "You sound quite warlike to-day, General."

"The snow—frozen!" announced Peter.

"Oh, now I can go to the grandmother!" rejoiced Heidi who was quick to understand Peter's odd way of expressing himself. "But why didn't you come to school? You could easily have come in the sledge."

"Took me too far down," said Peter. "So it was too late."

"Now that's what I'd call desertion," said the uncle, "and people who do that get their ears pulled; do you hear?"

Peter fidgeted uncomfortably for there was no one whom he feared and respected more than the Alm-Uncle.

"And a leader like you should be doubly ashamed of himself," continued the uncle. "What would you do if your goats ran anywhere they liked?"

"Beat them," Peter replied smartly.

"And if a boy behaved like that and got a good beating, what would you say then?"

"Serves him right," was the answer.

"Very well, then, if it should happen again that your sledge passes the school when you should be inside, come to me and get what you deserve!"

At last the meaning of the uncle's little speech was beginning to dawn on Peter. He looked quite thunder-struck and retreated into a corner. But the uncle said cheerfully, "Come now and eat with us and then Heidi can go up with you. In the evening you can bring her home again and have your supper here."

This unexpected turn to the conversation cheered Peter immensely. He obeyed at once and sat beside Heidi who could hardly eat for excitement about going to the grandmother's.

She ran to the cupboard and brought out the little warm coat with the hood which Clara had given her. Putting it on she stood waiting beside Peter and as soon as he had swallowed his last bite she said, "Come along now!"

When they arrived at the cottage, Peter's mother was alone in the room. She told them that the grandmother was not very well and had had to stay in bed because it was so cold. Heidi had always been accustomed to seeing the grandmother in her place in the corner. She ran into the other room and there lay the old woman in her narrow bed with only a thin coverlet over her but wrapped in the warm grey shawl.

"Thank God!" exclaimed the old woman when she heard Heidi running in for she had had a secret fear that the gentleman from Frankfurt, about whom Peter had spoken, would take the child away.

"Are you very ill, Grandmother?" asked Heidi with concern.

"No, no, child!" said the old woman and patted Heidi lovingly. "It is only the frost getting into my bones a little."

"Will you be better as soon as it is warm again?" Heidi persisted.

"Yes, yes, and with God's help before that so that I can get back to my spinning," said the grandmother, noticing how worried the child was.

This cheered Heidi a little; then she said thoughtfully, "Grandmother, in Frankfurt people put on a shawl when they go for a walk. Did you think it was for going to bed?"

"I have put the shawl on in bed to keep warm, Heidi. You see the cover is rather thin."

"But, Grandmother," Heidi started again, "your pillow goes downhill instead of uphill!"

"Yes, I know, child." The grandmother tried to find a more comfortable place on the thin pillow which looked as hard as a board. "You see, the pillow has never been particularly soft and now I have slept on it for so many years that it has become quite flat."

"If only I had asked Clara if I could take my bed

home! I had three big, thick pillows and they were so high I could hardly sleep for my head slipping off them. Could you have slept on them, Grandmother?"

"I am sure I could. One keeps warmer that way and breathes more easily when the head is high. However, don't let's speak about it. I have so much for which to thank God. The nice rolls I get, and the lovely warm shawl, and you coming to see me, Heidi. Would you care to read to me to-day?"

Heidi got down the old hymn book and chose the most beautiful verses. As the grandmother listened, a joyous smile lightened her face which had looked so worn and tired before.

Heidi stopped. "Grandmother, are you feeling better already?" she asked.

"Yes, child, I am much better already. Please read to the end."

After a while the child said: "I must go home now, Grandmother. It is getting late. I am so glad you are feeling better."

Heidi said good-bye to the grandmother and she and Peter set off quickly, for the darkness was already coming down. As Peter got out his sledge the moon came through and shone brightly on the white snow so that it seemed as if the day were about to break. Peter sat in front and Heidi behind, and off they shot down the Alm like two birds.

That night, as Heidi lay in her warm bed behind the stove, she thought about the grandmother and how she would like to visit her every day. But Heidi knew one or two weeks might pass before she was allowed to go up again. She thought and thought about how things could be arranged. Suddenly she had an idea and she could hardly wait for daylight to carry out her plan.

When she had prayed from the bottom of her heart for the grandfather and the grandmother and all the people she knew, she lay down on the soft hay and slept soundly and peacefully until the morning.

CHAPTER 19

Winter Continues

◆◆◆◆◆◆

EXT MORNING, Peter turned up at school in good
time. As was his usual habit when he happened
to be at school he paid a visit afterwards to the
uncle. To-day, immediately he entered the house, Heidi
rushed to him. "Peter, I have thought of something!"
she exclaimed.

"What is it?" he asked.

"You must learn to read now," was her reply.

"I know how to read—a little."

"Yes, yes, Peter, but I mean so well that you can read
easily and quickly."

"I'll never be able to do that," remarked Peter
gloomily.

"I don't believe that, and neither would anybody else,"
said Heidi with determination. "I shall teach you. I
know quite well how to do it. You must learn now and
then you will be able to read one or two hymns to
Grandmother every day."

"Oh, I don't care about *that* !" Peter grumbled.

This obstinacy towards something which she considered was kind and right annoyed Heidi. With flashing
eyes she stood before the boy and said threateningly,
"Then I will tell you what will happen if you refuse to
learn. Your mother has said already that she will send
you to Frankfurt to be taught and I have seen the
building where the boys go to school. Clara showed it
to me. But they don't go there just when they are boys,

148

but always, even when they are grown up. And don't think there is only one teacher as in our school."

A cold shudder ran down Peter's back.

"And you will have to go there among all the teachers and pupils," Heidi continued, "and if you cannot even read, and make mistakes with your spelling, you'll see how much they will laugh at you; much worse than Tinette, and if you only knew what she was like!"

"All right, then. I will," said Peter reluctantly.

Heidi was mollified at once. "That's right. We can start to-day," she decided joyfully. She dragged Peter to the table and brought out the necessary books. In Clara's big parcel there had been a book which Heidi thought was just right for teaching Peter, for it was an A B C book with verses.

They both bent over the book and the lesson began. Peter had to spell out the first verse again and again for Heidi wanted him to be able to read it correctly and fluently. At last she said, "You still don't know the verse so I shall read it to you. If you know the meaning it will be easier for you to spell it." And Heidi read:

"Learn A B C without a grudge
Or you'll be brought before the judge."

"I won't," said Peter obstinately.

"What?" asked Heidi.

"Go before the judge," was the answer.

"Hurry up then and learn these three letters and you won't need to."

Peter started again and repeated the three letters until Heidi said, "Now you can read these three!"

As she noticed the effect this verse had had upon Peter she thought it would be a good idea to prepare him a little for the following lessons.

"Wait! I'll read the other verses to you now," she continued, "and you'll see what else can happen. " And she began to read very slowly and clearly:

"D E F G must smoothly flow
Or you will get a nasty blow.

If you forget H I J K
The fatal blow will fall to-day.

To learn L M is not a strain
And will prevent a lot of pain.

Remember well N O P Q
Or you'll get what's in store for you.

R S T may save a smack
If you will make a quick attack."

Here Heidi stopped because Peter was so quiet. All these secret hints and threats had petrified him with fright and he stared anxiously at Heidi. Her kind heart was touched at once and she said reassuringly, "You don't need to be afraid, Peter. If you come every evening and learn as well as you have done to-day you will soon know the letters and nothing will happen to you. But you must come *every* day and not just sometimes as you did with school—even if it snows. The snow doesn't trouble you anyway."

Peter promised. Fear of punishment had made him quite docile. Then he set off home.

He followed Heidi's advice and arrived promptly every evening. The letters were studied with zeal and the verses taken to heart. Often the grandfather listened to the lessons while he contentedly smoked his pipe.

Every now and then his face would twitch with amusement. Peter was usually asked to stay to supper with them which was a great compensation to him for the anxiety which the verses caused.

So the winter passed. Peter appeared regularly and made good progress. He had now got as far as U and Heidi read :

> "Who still mistakes the U for V
> May go where he won't like to be."

This gave Peter an uncomfortable feeling but made him learn all the quicker lest the threat were carried out. The following evening the verse was:

> "If W is still unknown
> The stick may come into its own."

Peter remarked sneeringly, "There isn't one."

But Heidi reminded him that the grandfather had a very big stick in his cupboard, and this made him bend over his W in a feverish effort to memorise it.

The next day the book said:

> "X is a cross you may recall
> And this is easiest of them all."

And Heidi quickly prompted him to learn another letter as well so that only the last one remained for the following day. Although Peter tried to object, Heidi read out:

> "To stop at Y will never do
> And all the world will laugh at you."

Peter at once attacked the Y with energy and did not give

up until he could close his eyes and still remember what it looked like.

Peter arrived the next day feeling very jaunty because there was only one more letter to be learnt and when Heidi read the verse:

"Who still forgets the Z you know
    Straight to the Hottentots will go,"

he said sarcastically, "Who knows where they live?"

"Grandfather does. Wait! I shall ask him at once. He is only across the road with the pastor."

Heidi was about to run to the door when Peter exclaimed in alarm, "Wait a moment!" In his imagination he saw both the pastor and the uncle carrying him off and sending him away to the Hottentots—because he really had forgotten completely what Z was like.

"What is the matter?" Heidi asked in surprise.

"Nothing! Come back! I shall learn now," muttered Peter. And from day to day Peter made progress with his reading.

The ice had thawed and new snow had fallen every day so that about three weeks had passed since Heidi's visit to the grandmother. This made her work all the harder with Peter so that he would be able to take her place and read to the old woman.

One evening Peter went home and announced, "I can do it now!"

"What can you do, Peter," asked his mother.

"Read," he answered.

"Do you really mean it? Did you hear that, Grandmother?" Brigitta exclaimed.

Grandmother did hear and was wondering how this had come about.

"I have to read a hymn now. Heidi said so."

Brigitta quickly fetched the book and the grand-mother smiled in anticipation of hearing the comfort-ing words once more. Peter sat down and began to read and his mother sat beside him, listening, and saying after each verse, in a voice full of astonishment and admiration, "Who would have thought it!"

The grandmother, too, followed the verses with the greatest attention but she did not say anything.

The following day at school, when it came Peter's turn to read, the teacher said, "Well, Peter, must we pass you again or would you like to try?"

Without hesitation, Peter read three lines. The teacher laid down his book and stared at Peter as if he had never seen him before. Then he said, "Peter, this is a miracle! With all the patience in the world I did not succeed in teaching you even your letters and here you are reading beautifully. How did this come about?"

"It was Heidi," Peter answered.

In surprise the teacher turned towards Heidi who sat on her bench looking as though nothing out of the ordinary had happened.

The teacher continued, "Altogether I have noticed a change in you. You have been attending school very regularly lately. What can have brought about this change for the better?"

"The uncle," came the reply.

With ever-growing astonishment the teacher looked at Heidi, then back again at Peter.

As soon as school was over, the teacher hastened to tell the pastor what had happened and what a good influence the uncle and Heidi had been.

Every night now Peter read a hymn in obedience to Heidi's instructions, but he refused to read a second one and indeed the grandmother never encouraged him to do so.

Brigitta was always delighted that her Peter had achieved so much but the grandmother said, "Yes, it is good that he has learnt so well but still I shall be glad when it is spring and Heidi can come up again. When Peter reads there always seem to be some words missing in the hymns so that I don't understand them so well as when Heidi reads them."

The reason was, of course, that Peter was rather lazy about reading for the grandmother and if a word were too difficult or too long he just skipped over it thinking it would not matter very much to the grandmother seeing there were so many words!

CHAPTER 20

News from Clara

~~~~~~~~

MAY HAD COME again and from the heights the streamlets rippled eagerly down into the valley. The last snow had melted and the golden sun had dried up the last traces of winter. Heidi was happy to be on the Alm again and jumped about for joy, and it seemed to her that the little wild creatures which darted about were as happy as she and all were humming and singing, "On the Alm! On the Alm!"

Familiar sounds came from the carpenter's shed. The grandfather was busy finishing a beautiful new chair and another one, already finished, stood outside.

"Oh, I know what these are for!" cried Heidi. "We will need them when they come from Frankfurt. This one is for Grandmamma and the one you are making now is for Clara."

Suddenly there was a great whistling and shouting and Heidi knew immediately it was Peter. There he stood brandishing a letter. It was addressed to Heidi. Carefully she read the address then ran towards the grandfather, holding out her letter. "From Frankfurt! From Clara! Do you want to hear it?"

Of course, both he and Peter wanted to hear it, so Heidi began to read:

"DEAR HEIDI,

"Everything is packed and ready and in two or three days we shall be on our way. The doctor comes to see me every day and as he comes into the room he

155

always calls, 'Off you go now! Off to the Alm as quickly as you can!' He says everybody must become healthy and happy there. He, too, is his own self again after being with you. Oh, how I am looking forward to seeing everything, to being with you and also to getting to know Peter and the goats! I can hardly bear to wait. Good-bye, Heidi! Grandmamma sends her love.

"Your affectionate friend,

"CLARA."

Peter was not at all thrilled with the news of the arrival of the guests from Frankfurt. It made him very cross indeed. But Heidi was overflowing with happiness. As soon as possible she called at the grandmother's to tell her the good news. The grandmother was sitting spinning once more in her usual corner. She was no longer confined to bed, but although she was so much better her face wore an expression of sadness. Peter had told her the news about the people who were coming from Frankfurt and the grandmother had her own ideas of what might come to pass. She could not help dreading that they might take Heidi away again.

As Heidi was in the midst of telling her the great news she had to stop suddenly and ask with concern, "What is the matter, Grandmother? Aren't you happy about all this?"

"Yes, yes, I am glad for you, Heidi," said the old woman, trying to put on a more cheerful expression. She was anxious to hide her fears and suggested, "I know something, Heidi, that would calm my thoughts. Read the hymn for me which begins:

'All things together work for good
For those who trust in Me.'"

Heidi quickly found the hymn and when she had finished reading the grandmother said, " Yes, that is right! If one trusts in God one knows that whatever happens is for our good. Read it once more so that we won't forget."

The month of May had seldom before been so beautiful and sunny, and the grandfather exclaimed repeatedly, "This is indeed a good year. The sun will make the plants grow strong and nourishing. Take care, Peter, that your flock doesn't get out of hand from overfeeding!"

Peter's answer could be clearly read in his face. "I can manage them!"

May had passed and June was drawing to its close when one morning Heidi ran out of the hut. Just as she turned the corner she gave a loud cry which brought the uncle hurrying to see what had happened.

"Grandfather! Grandfather!" the child called excitedly, "Come over here! Come and look!"

He came, and his eyes followed the direction of her outstretched arm. A strange procession could be seen coming up the mountain path. In front came two men carrying a sedan chair in which a young girl sat, wrapped in many shawls. A horse followed, mounted by a stately lady who looked about her with keen interest. Another man pushed an empty wheel-chair, for it was easier and safer to carry the invalid up the mountain in the sedan.

"Here they are! Here they are!" cried Heidi joyfully.

When the eagerly expected guests reached the Alm, Heidi sprang forward and the two children embraced each other lovingly. Grandmamma, too, was welcomed with the greatest affection. Then Grandmamma turned to the Alm-Uncle who came forward to bid them welcome. They all felt like old friends, as they had heard so much about each other.

Grandmamma was delighted with the beautiful

situation. "And how well my little Heidi is looking!" she remarked, patting the child's rosy cheeks. "What do *you* think, Clara? Isn't it delightful here?"

Clara was entranced. Never in her life before had she seen or imagined anything so beautiful. "Oh, how lovely it is! How I wish I could always live here, Grandmamma!"

Meantime the uncle had pushed the invalid chair nearer and now he suggested, "Wouldn't it be better to put the little daughter into her accustomed seat?" And without waiting for assistance he lifted Clara in his strong arms and very gently placed her in her own comfortable chair, putting some of the wraps over her knees and doing it all as expertly as if he had looked after invalids all his life. Grandmamma was greatly impressed by his care and attention.

Clara could not find words to express her delight in everything around her. "Oh, Heidi," she said, "if only I could go about and see all the things you have described to me!"

With a great effort Heidi succeeded in wheeling the chair on to the grass so that Clara could see the magnificent old fir trees which had gazed down undisturbed for so many years on the valley below. Heidi opened the door of the goat-house so that Clara could see inside.

"If only I could wait till Peter comes with the goats!" Clara said regretfully. "How I should love to see Little Swan and Little Bear! If we must always leave so early as you say, Grandmamma, we shall never see them!"

"My dear child, let us enjoy the things we can and not think of those we may miss."

"Oh, how pretty the flowers are! If only I could get up and pick some!"

Heidi ran and gathered a big bunch. "But that is nothing, Clara," she said. "If you come with us up to

the pasture you will see ever so many. There they are as
thick as a carpet and if you sit down amongst them you
never want to get up again."

Heidi's eyes sparkled with longing to be able to show
it all to her friend and Clara's soft blue eyes reflected
Heidi's enthusiasm.

"Oh, Grandmamma! Do you think I shall ever be
allowed to go up as high as that?" she asked. "If only
I could go with you, Heidi! I should like to climb all over
the Alm."

"I shall push your chair," said Heidi stoutly, and to
show how easy it was she made a rush at the chair which
nearly sent it rolling down the slope. But the grandfather
was near at hand and stopped it in time.

Grandfather had been busy preparing the meal and
he had brought the table and the chairs outside beside the
bench. Soon the meal was ready and the whole company
sat down merrily. Grandmamma was delighted with this
dining-room under the blue sky where she could sit and
enjoy the magnificent view far down into the valley.
"Is it really true?" she exclaimed when she saw Clara
taking a second helping of toasted cheese which she was
eating with a great appetite.

"Yes, Grandmamma. It tastes so good. Better than
the whole menu at Ragatz," Clara assured her.

"That's right. Eat all you can," encouraged the
uncle. "Our mountain air makes up for the deficiency
of the kitchen."

Grandmamma and the uncle chatted together as
though they had known each other for years. They had
much in common and the time passed quickly in lively
conversation. But suddenly Grandmamma remembered,
"We will have to go presently, Clara. The sun will be
going down soon and the men with the chair will be
here."

"Just let's stay another hour, Grandmamma," pleaded Clara. "We haven't seen inside the cottage yet and we must see Heidi's bed."

Grandmamma wanted to see inside the cottage, too, and the uncle invited them to go in. Clara's chair, however, was too broad to pass through the door, but without hesitation, the uncle lifted Clara out of the chair and carried her inside.

Grandmamma looked around with interest and was very much impressed by the tidiness and cosy atmosphere of the house. "Is your bed up there, Heidi?" she asked and started to climb up to the loft. "Oh, what a lovely scent! This should be a healthy bedroom," she exclaimed.

Grandfather followed, carrying Clara, and Heidi came after. They all stood around Heidi's bed. "Heidi, how jolly!" exclaimed Clara. "From your bed you can look straight up into the sky! And you will always have the lovely smell of the hay and will be able to listen to the fir trees rustling!"

The uncle looked at Grandmamma. "I have an idea," he said. "I think if we could agree to have your little grand-daughter staying here with us for a while she would be bound to get strong and well. With all the rugs you have brought we could make a fine soft bed and I myself would look after her."

Clara and Heidi were as happy as two birds let out of their cage at this suggestion and the Grandmamma's face beamed. " My dear Uncle, you are kindness itself," she said. "I have just been thinking how good a holiday so high up in the mountains would be for the child. But the nursing, the trouble and the inconvenience for you! And you make the offer as if it were nothing at all. I thank you from the bottom of my heart." The old lady took his hand and the uncle nodded happily.

He at once started to get Clara's bed ready and he and the Grandmamma spread the rugs over it. When they had finished, the bed was so smooth and thick, not a single bit of hay could penetrate. Satisfied, Grandmamma climbed down the ladder and joined the children who were already discussing how they would spend their time. But, how long would Clara be allowed to stay, was the great question. Grandmamma replied, "Grandfather knows best. You must ask him."

The grandfather thought four weeks would be just right to decide if the mountain air was agreeing with the child. The prospect of being together for so long surpassed the children's expectations and they both shouted for joy.

The chair-bearers appeared at the cottage but they were immediately sent down the mountain again.

"It is not farewell, Grandmamma," said Clara as they parted. "You will come and visit us here on the Alm and see what we are doing and how we are getting on, won't you?"

Heidi could only express her happiness with a high jump.

The day closed for Clara with the most overwhelming experience of all. She lay in the big soft bed in the loft with Heidi near her and looked through the round, open window right into the middle of the star-lit sky. "Oh, Heidi!" she exclaimed. "It seems as if we were riding through the sky!"

"Do you know why the stars twinkle so happily?" asked Heidi.

"No, why do you think?"

"Because they see how well God has arranged everything for men so that nobody needs to be afraid and can be quite sure that everything will turn out for the best.

But we must not forget to pray, Clara, and to ask God to remember us."

The children sat up and said their prayers together; then Heidi put her head on her arm and fell asleep at once. But Clara lay awake a long time. She had never been able to see the stars at home because she had never been outside the house at night, and inside, the heavy curtains were always drawn long before the stars came out. So she could not gaze long enough at the sparkling heavens and lay looking out of the little round window until at last her eyes closed of their own accord.

CHAPTER 21

Life on the Alm

~~~~~~

THE Alm-Uncle had been standing outside the hut as was his habit, watching the early mists rising and the new day awakening. The morning clouds grew brighter and brighter until the sun appeared in its full glory and flooded the rocks, woods and mountains with golden light.

The uncle went back into the hut and quietly climbed up the little ladder. Clara had just opened her eyes and did not know at first where she was. Then she saw the sleeping Heidi beside her and heard the kindly voice of the grandfather whispering, "Did you sleep well?"

Clara assured him that she had slept soundly all night. Now Heidi was awake and watched the grandfather carry Clara downstairs. Quickly she got up and dressed and ran down the ladder after them and out into the open air.

A fresh breeze blew across the children's faces and Clara lay back in her chair with a feeling of comfort and health. Every breath was a joy in this pure mountain air. She had never imagined that the Alm would be so beautiful.

"Oh, Heidi, if only I could stay in the mountains with you always!" she exclaimed.

"Do you understand now why I said that the best place in the world is on the Alm with Grandfather?"

Just at that moment the grandfather appeared with two bowls of foaming milk. "This will give you strength," he said to Clara.

Clara had never tasted goats' milk before and she smelt it first. But when she saw Heidi drinking hers to the last drop, she did the same. It tasted sweet and strong, as though it contained sugar and cinnamon. Soon her bowl was empty, too.

"To-morrow we may be able to take two?" the grandfather suggested, observing with satisfaction how Clara had followed Heidi's example.

Soon Peter arrived with his flock and the uncle took him aside to tell him to be sure to take Little Swan high up where she would get the best grass. "Why are you staring over there as though you wanted to eat somebody?" the grandfather exclaimed in the midst of his instructions. "Now be off! And remember what I have said!"

Peter marched off at once, but it was obvious that there was something going on in his mind. When Heidi appeared amongst the goats he said to her threateningly, "You had better come with me because Little Swan has to get special attention."

"No, I can't," replied Heidi. "I can't come so long as Clara is with me. But Grandfather has promised that sometime we shall come together."

As she said this she ran back to Clara and Peter made threatening gestures towards the invalid chair. Then he quickly climbed up until he was out of sight for he was afraid the uncle might have seen him.

Clara and Heidi had so many plans that they hardly knew what to do first. Heidi suggested that they should first write to Grandmamma for they had promised to write every day and tell her all their experiences.

"Must we write the letter inside the cottage?" asked Clara who preferred to stay outside and enjoy the lovely scenery.

Heidi went into the cottage to get all the things they

needed and then they both settled down to write the letter. After almost every sentence Clara had to stop and look round. It was far too beautiful for writing. The wind was no longer cool, and gently caressed her face. Insects danced and hummed in the air and a deep silence lay on the sunny fields. The whole, broad valley lay peacefully below and only now and then was the silence broken by the yodelling of a shepherd boy, and the sound echoed softly amongst the rocks.

The morning passed so quickly, the children were surprised to see the uncle bringing the lunch which they took out of doors just as they had done the day before. In the afternoon they sat in the shadow of the fir trees and Clara related all the things that had happened in Frankfurt since Heidi left.

Evening was approaching and the goats came rushing down the mountain, their keeper following them with a not very pleasant expression on his face. He did not even answer the children's friendly call but went on chasing the goats.

When Clara saw that the grandfather had taken Little Swan away for milking she suddenly felt very impatient to taste the milk. "Isn't it strange!" she said. "I never used to like to eat. Everything tasted like cod liver oil, and now I can hardly wait until supper-time when Grandfather brings the milk."

This time Clara even finished her milk before Heidi and asked the grandfather for a second helping. He nodded cheerfully, and taking both bowls, went back into the cottage. When he returned with the milk he brought two large slices of bread, spread with plenty of butter which he had got fresh from a herdsman's cottage that afternoon. It tasted delicious and the grandfather smiled with satisfaction to see the two children eat so heartily.

That night, when they went to bed, Clara wanted to look up again at the stars but her eyes would not stay open and she was soon fast asleep like Heidi and slept as she had never done before in her life.

So the days passed happily. One day the children were surprised to see two porters climbing up the mountain. Each of them carried a bed on his back, complete with sheets and mattress. The men also brought a letter from Grandmamma in which she said that the beds were for Clara and Heidi. She also thanked the children for their letters and encouraged them to continue to write and tell her about everything that happened.

Grandmamma was very pleased that Clara was enjoying the Alm so much and she was quite content to wait a little before she repeated her visit to the Alm because the ride up the steep mountain was rather trying for her.

Clara had now spent three weeks on the Alm. During the last few days, when Grandfather carried her downstairs to put her into her chair he had asked her, "Wouldn't the little daughter like to try to stand on the ground?" Clara had always tried to please him but had soon been forced to cry out, "Oh, it hurts!" and had clung to him; but each day he allowed her to stand just a little longer without her noticing.

For years they had not had such a splendid summer on the Alm. Every day the sun shone brilliantly out of a cloudless sky.

Heidi never tired of describing the high pasture to her friend. As she told Clara about the lovely rock roses and the vivid blue harebells she longed suddenly to be up there once again and she sprang up and asked the grandfather, "Will you come to the pasture with us to-morrow?"

He consented. "But the little daughter must do me

a favour too. To-night she must try her very best to stand."

Cheerfully Heidi ran with this news to Clara who promised to try to stand on her feet as much as ever. Grandfather wanted, for she was looking forward immensely to this excursion.

As soon as Heidi caught sight of Peter in the evening she exclaimed, "Peter! Peter! To-morrow we shall come up too and stay all day on the pasture."

But Peter just grumbled like a bear in a temper.

That night Clara and Heidi went to their new beds full of anticipation of the next day. They agreed to stay awake all night to talk about their plans, but hardly had their heads touched the pillows when the conversation suddenly ceased. Clara saw in her dreams a big pasture thickly covered with flowers and Heidi heard the eagle crying, "Come! Come! Come!"

CHAPTER 22

An Unexpected Event

~~~~~~~~

EARLY NEXT morning the old man looked out to see what sort of day it would be. The dark shadows in the valley lifted and gradually a rosy light spread across the mountains until above and below were bathed in colour. The sun had risen.

The uncle brought the invalid chair from the shed and placed it in front of the house, and then went inside to tell the children what a beautiful morning it was.

Peter came lumbering up the hill. All the jealousy and temper in him had reached a climax. For weeks he had not had Heidi to himself. When he came in the morning the strange child was carried out to her chair and Heidi's attention was completely taken up with her. In the evening, the invalid was still there and again Heidi had no time for him. Not once, all during the summer, had Heidi come up to the pasture, and though she came to-day she would still be accompanied by her friend and would still have no time for him. Peter anticipated this and it made him quite wild with rage.

When he caught sight of the chair, standing so proudly on its wheels, it seemed to him that here was the enemy who had done all this harm to him and would, to-day, hurt him still more. There was no one about and everything was quiet. Wildly he rushed forward, and, seizing the chair, he pushed it with all his might down the slope. He pushed with such violence that it disappeared almost at once. Peter then rushed up the Alm and took cover behind a big blackberry bush. Here he was hidden from sight of the uncle but could watch the chair's progress down the mountain. Far below, he saw it turn over and over and fly into a hundred pieces. The sight filled Peter with such an indescribable joy that he laughed aloud and stamped his feet. The boy raced round in circles, completely beside himself at the destruction of his enemy.

And now he thought of all the pleasant things for him which would result from the disaster. The stranger would have to leave because she could not get about without her chair; then Heidi would be free again to come with him up to the pasture. Everything would be as it had been in days gone by. It did not occur to Peter that if we do something wrong, trouble is sure to follow.

Presently Heidi came out and ran to the shed. The door was wide open. She looked everywhere, puzzled to know what had become of the chair.

"Did you move the chair, Heidi?" asked the grandfather.

"I have looked everywhere for it. You said it was by the door," replied Heidi.

The wind suddenly grew stronger and rattled the door of the shed, blowing it back against the wall with a bang.

"Grandfather, it must have been the wind," called Heidi. "Oh, if it has blown the chair down the valley we will never get it back in time."

"If it has rolled as far as that we will never get it back at all," said the grandfather. "By now it will be in a thousand pieces," and he went round the corner of the hut to look down the path.

"Oh, what a pity! Now we can't go," lamented Clara. "If I have no chair I am sure I shall have to go home. Oh, what a pity!"

"We will go to-day as we intended," replied the uncle. "Then we shall see what else can be done."

The children were delighted.

The uncle then went back into the hut and bringing out some of the rugs, spread them out on the sunniest spot for Clara to sit on. Then he brought the milk for the children and led Little Swan and Little Bear out of the shed.

"I wonder why the boy is not here yet?" thought the uncle.

He picked up Clara and, carrying her on one arm and the rugs on the other he said, "Now, let's be off! The goats will come with us."

With one arm round Little Swan's neck and the other round Little Bear's, Heidi walked behind the grandfather.

When they arrived on the pasture they saw here and there on the slopes, goats peacefully grazing, and in the midst of them, on the ground, Peter was lying.

"I'll teach you to pass my house another time, you lazy fellow!" called the uncle. "What does this mean?"

Peter shot up at the sound of the familiar voice. "There was nobody up," he answered.

"Did you see anything of the chair?" the uncle continued.

"Of what?" Peter answered back obstinately.

The uncle said no more but spread the rugs on the sunny slope and set Clara down upon them, asking if she was comfortable.

"As comfortable as in the chair," she said gratefully, "and I think this must be the most beautiful spot on earth. Oh, Heidi, how lovely it is!"

The grandfather got ready to leave them. "Enjoy yourselves!" he said. "When dinner-time comes, Heidi will get the food from the rucksack which I have put in the shade. Peter will provide the milk and in the evening

I will come back to fetch you. Now I must go and look for the chair and see what has happened to it."

The children had never been so happy together. The goats would gather round them in a friendly way and they had even got to know Clara well enough to rub their heads affectionately against her shoulder.

So the hours went by, and Heidi thought she would like to go to her favourite spot where the flowers grew so profusely, and see if the cups were open now and as beautiful as last year. Clara could only be taken there in the evening when the grandfather came back, but by that time the flower bells would have closed again. Heidi could not resist the temptation to go and look. Hesitatingly she asked Clara, "Do you mind, Clara, if I leave you for a few minutes? I would so much like to go and see the flowers. But wait!" Heidi had an idea. She led Snowflake up to Clara. "There, now! You won't be lonely."

Clara encouraged Heidi to go. She was quite content to be with the little goat. Heidi had thrown some leaves into Clara's lap and Clara held them out to Snowflake one by one. The little goat ate the leaves slowly from her hands. As she sat alone on the mountain and looked at the little animal which seemed to look up to her for protection, she thought how wonderful it would be to be able, one day, to help others instead of always being dependent as she was now.

Heidi reached the lovely flower patch and the ground seemed to be completely covered with sparkling gold. It was more beautiful than ever and she breathed in the sweet fragrance. Suddenly she turned and ran back to Clara, out of breath with excitement. "You must come and see it!" she called from a distance. "The flowers are so beautiful now and in the evening they may have changed. I can carry you, don't you think, Clara?"

Clara shook her head. "No, no, Heidi! You are much smaller than I. Oh, if only I could walk!"

Heidi looked about as if searching for something. Up above, Peter sat staring at the children, as if he couldn't believe his eyes. Didn't he destroy the hated chair so that the stranger would not be able to move about and here she sat beside Heidi? Heidi spotted Peter and called, "Come down, Peter!"

"No, I don't want to," was the reply.

"But you must! Come! I can't carry Clara by myself. You have to help me. Come quickly!" Heidi urged him.

"I don't want to," he shouted again.

Heidi came up the hill towards him. With flaming eyes she stood before him and said, "Peter, if you don't come at once I shall do something which you won't like at all, I can tell you!"

Fear seized Peter. He knew he had done something wicked which he did not want anybody to know about and here was Heidi speaking as though she knew all about it. What if she told the uncle! Peter feared nobody so much as him. Tortured with anxiety, he got up and went down to Heidi.

"I am coming, but you mustn't do what you said," he pleaded timidly so that Heidi felt quite sorry for him.

"There's nothing to be afraid of. Come with me now."

Heidi told him to take Clara's arm and she would support her from the other side. But the difficulty was how to make her walk when she could not even stand. So Heidi ordered Peter to give her his arm to lean on and asked her to put her other arm firmly round Heidi's neck. "Then we can carry you."

But Peter had never in his life before given his arm to anybody and kept it stiffly by his body.

"That's not the way," said Heidi and showed him how to do it.

But in spite of it all they did not get on very well. Clara was not light and the team was too unequal— down on the one side and up on the other. Clara tried to help by putting forward first one foot and then the other but she always drew them back quickly again.

"Put your foot down firmly," Heidi suggested.

"Do you think——" Clara hesitated.

But she obeyed, and ventured first one step on the ground and then another. The pain made her moan a little. Then she put a foot out again and cried joyfully that it was less painful already.

"Try again!" urged Heidi eagerly.

Clara went on trying, again and again, and suddenly she exclaimed, "I can do it, Heidi! Oh, I can! Look! I can make steps—one after the other!"

"Can you really walk now? If only Grandfather were here!" cried Heidi.

Clara had still to hold on to both Peter and Heidi, but with every step she felt safer.

Heidi was quite beside herself with joy. "Now we will be able to come here every day and you will be able to walk like me and you will be healthy!"

It was not far to the slope where the beautiful flowers grew. The children could already see the yellow and blue patches. Soon they reached it.

"Let's sit down here," said Clara. They sat down in the midst of the flowers. Heidi thought she had never seen it so beautiful before. Clara was silent, overcome with happiness at the beauty around her and at the wonderful prospect which had opened up before her . . . the joy of being able to walk about like other people. Peter was quiet, too, and lay quite still on the ground. He was fast asleep.

The children remained there for a long time. It was long past noon when some of the goats approached the slope and started to bleat loudly. The chorus awoke Peter and he remembered with a pang of misgiving his wicked deed of the morning. He willingly obeyed Heidi's every command in the hope that she would not report him to the uncle. The three of them went back to the pasture and had their meal, and although Peter ate up every bit as usual he did not enjoy it very much, tortured as he was by the fear of punishment.

Soon after they had finished, the grandfather appeared, climbing up the slope, and Heidi rushed towards him to tell him the good news. The grandfather's face brightened and he smiled happily at Clara. "You have made the effort and you have won," he said.

He lifted Clara up and with his left arm behind her she walked, with his strong support, much more confidently than before. Heidi skipped happily beside them. Then the grandfather lifted Clara into his arms. "We mustn't overdo it," he said. "In any case it is time to go home."

Later in the evening, when Peter arrived in Dorfli with his goats a crowd of people had gathered. They were looking at something which lay on the ground. Peter wanted to see too, and eventually elbowed his way through. There lay the pitiful remains of Clara's chair.

"I saw them carry it up," said the baker. "I bet it's worth a lot of money. I wonder if somebody did this deliberately. When the gentleman from Frankfurt hears of this he is sure to investigate. Suspicion is going to fall on all those who have been up on the Alm lately. I'm glad I haven't been up there for two years at least."

Peter had heard enough. Stealthily he crept away from the crowd and ran up the mountain path as though the devil were after him. When he reached home he did not take any supper but went straight off to bed; but he found no peace there, either, for he expected the police to arrive at any moment and carry him off to prison in Frankfurt.

As the children lay in bed that night, looking out at the stars, Heidi said, "I have been thinking all day how good it is that God does not give us just what we ask. He always knows of something better for us."

"Why do you think that, Heidi?" asked Clara.

"Because when I was in Frankfurt I prayed to be allowed to go home at once and when it did not happen I thought God did not hear. But, you see, if I had run away at once you would never have come here and would never have got well."

Clara thought hard. "But, Heidi," she said, "that would mean that we must never pray for anything because God knows better than we do."

"Yes, Clara, but we must do it like this," Heidi replied eagerly. "Every day we must thank God for everything to let Him know that we haven't forgotten that it all comes from Him. But, you know, if we don't get what we have asked for we must not think that God has not heard, and stop praying. We must say then, 'Now I know, dear Father, that you have something better in mind and I am glad that you will make it right in the end.'"

"How well you can explain it, Heidi," remarked Clara.

"Grandmamma explained it all to me and it all turned out to be true. But I think we have to thank God particularly to-day because He has given us this great happiness—that you can walk now."

The following morning, the grandfather suggested that they should invite the grandmamma to the Alm because they had something new to show her. But the children wanted to give Grandmamma a great surprise and wanted to wait until Clara could go for a little walk supported only by Heidi. They thought it would be about a week before this could happen and in their next letter Grandmamma was eagerly invited to come for a visit; but they did not give away the secret.

Every day walking became easier and less painful for Clara and longer walks were undertaken. The exercise gave her such an appetite that the grandfather had to cut the bread a little bit thicker every day, and he was very pleased when he saw it disappearing.

So another week went by, and the day of the grandmamma's visit approached.

CHAPTER 23

Promises to Meet Again

━━━━━

THE GRANDMAMMA wrote to announce the day of her arrival and Peter brought the letter up from Dorfli that morning. He handed it apprehensively to the Alm-Uncle and then turned quickly and fled back down the mountain.

"Grandfather," asked Heidi. "Why does Peter always behave now as if he expected to be punished for something? He is like the goats running away for fear of the stick."

"Maybe he, too, is afraid of the stick which he sometimes thoroughly deserves," replied the grandfather.

Heidi tidied the hut in preparation for the grandmamma's arrival, and when everything was in order the children sat down on the bench outside the cottage, ready to welcome her. The grandfather came and sat down beside them. He held in his hands a lovely bunch of gentians which he had picked that morning. Soon they saw a group of people toiling up the mountain path. First there came a guide, and then a white horse on which rode the grandmamma, and last of all a porter with grandmamma's luggage. At last the procession arrived and the old lady caught sight of the children.

"Why, what is this?" she cried out. "Clara, you aren't in your chair! I can't believe my eyes!" And before even shaking hands with any one she still exclaimed, "Clara, is this really you? Your cheeks have become quite round and rosy. I hardly recognise you, child."

She came forward to embrace Clara, but Heidi quickly

slipped from the bench, and, with Clara leaning on her shoulder, they walked slowly towards the grandmamma.

The old lady stood transfixed. Then she embraced her little grandchild, then Heidi, then Clara again. She gazed at them both speechlessly. At last she saw the Alm-Uncle who had been watching the proceedings with a broad smile. With Clara on her arm she walked with her to the bench, and, letting Clara sit down, she grasped the old man's hand.

"My dear Uncle! How can I thank you? This is your doing! Your care and nursing——"

"And God's sunshine and mountain air," interrupted the grandfather, smiling.

"And also Little Swan's good milk," put in Clara. "Grandmamma, you should have seen how much milk I have been drinking!"

"I can see it, Clara, by your cheeks! What a change! You have become plump and strong and taller, too. I simply can't take my eyes off you! But now we must send a telegram to my son in Paris. He must come at once—but I shan't tell him why. This will be the most wonderful surprise he has ever had. Uncle, have the men gone? How can we send a telegram?"

"They have gone, but, if you are in a hurry, I will call Peter. He will do it."

A piercing whistle summoned Peter and he came running down from the high rocks. He was given a piece of paper on which the message was written and the uncle told him to take it to the post office at Dorfli. Peter hurried away, quite relieved to see that no policeman had arrived so far.

In Paris, Herr Sesemann had finished his business and he also had a surprise in store. Without giving any warning, he took the train to Basle, for he had a great longing to see his little daughter from whom he had been separated all summer. He arrived at Ragatz a few hours after his mother's departure, and this fitted in nicely with his plans. He took a coach to Maienfeld, where he learned that he could drive as far as Dorfli. The climb from there seemed to him very long and fatiguing, and when the cottage failed to come into view he began to wonder uneasily if he had chosen the right path or if the hut was on the other side of the mountain. He looked around, but no human being was to be seen of whom he could ask the way. Just then, a boy came running from above; it was Peter with the telegram. He did not keep to the footpath but ran straight down the mountainside. Herr Sesemann beckoned to him and reluctantly Peter came forward.

"Come here, boy!" Herr Sesemann encouraged him. "Tell me, is this the way to the hut where the old man lives with the child, Heidi, and where the people from Frankfurt are staying now?"

A gasp was the only answer that came from Peter, and in his haste to get away, the boy fell head over heels and somersaulted down the mountainside, just as the chair had done—except that Peter did not fall to pieces! The telegram, however, was torn to scraps.

"What a timid boy!" exclaimed Herr Sesemann, thinking that the appearance of a stranger had had this extraordinary effect on the simple boy of the mountains. And he continued on his way.

Peter had been convinced that this was the policeman from Frankfurt. He tumbled on down the mountainside until at last he managed to catch hold of a bush. He had to lie still for a moment or two to recover, and then he picked himself up and scrambled back up the slope.

Shortly after meeting Peter, Herr Sesemann reached the first hut and knew that he was on the right road. So he climbed higher and higher and at last, after a long, strenuous walk, his goal came in sight. There stood the Alm hut.

Herr Sesemann joyfully climbed the last steep path. Before he had reached the top he was recognised by the party outside the cottage and quickly a surprise was prepared for him. As he left the path to approach the hut, two figures came towards him. A tall girl with fair hair and rosy cheeks leaned on her smaller companion. Herr Sesemann stood still and stared at them.

"Papa, don't you know me?" called Clara. "Have I changed so much?"

At once Herr Sesemann rushed to embrace his little daughter.

"Yes, you have changed indeed! Is it possible? Can this be my little Clara?" he exclaimed repeatedly.

Grandmamma had come forward. "My dear son, what do you think of this?" she cried. "You had prepared a pleasant surprise for us but I think we have an even pleasanter one for you! But now you must meet the Alm-Uncle who is our greatest benefactor."

"Gladly, and also our dear little Heidi," replied Herr Sesemann, shaking hands with Heidi. "I don't need to ask if you are well and happy. No alpine rose could look more blooming."

Heidi looked up with sparkling eyes at the kind Herr Sesemann who had always been so good to her. How glad she was that he could find such happiness on the Alm.

Then the grandmamma led her son to the Alm-Uncle. As the two men shook hands, Herr Sesemann expressed his heartfelt thanks and his great astonishment at the miracle.

Her eyes filled with tears, and the grandmamma turned away and looked towards the ancient fir trees. A patch of blue caught her eye. It was a beautiful bouquet of blue gentians. "How exquisite!" she exclaimed. "Heidi, did you pick them for me?"

"No," replied Heidi, "but I think I know who did."

Suddenly, a slight rustling sound came from behind the trees. It was Peter. At the sight of the strange gentleman with the Alm-Uncle, he had tried to slip away unobserved. But the grandmamma recognised him. "Come here, my boy," she said loudly. "Don't be afraid."

Paralysed with fright, Peter looked out from behind the trees. "It is all up now!" he thought. His face distorted with terror, he began to creep forward.

"Come along now," encouraged the grandmamma. "Now tell me, boy, did you do this?"

Peter never lifted his eyes and, of course, did not see where the grandmamma's finger pointed. All he had noticed was the uncle standing at the corner of the hut, looking piercingly at him, and, what was most terrifying of all, beside him stood the policeman from Frankfurt. Trembling all over, Peter could only mutter something which sounded like "Yes."

"Well, what is so dreadful about that?" asked the grandmamma.

"That it is broken to pieces and can't be put together again." With great difficulty Peter managed to stammer the words and his legs shook so much he could hardly stand.

Grandmamma went over to the Alm-Uncle. "My dear Uncle, is there something seriously wrong with the poor boy?" she asked sympathetically.

"Nothing," replied the uncle, " but I think the lad may have been the 'wind' which chased the invalid chair down the mountain and now he is expecting his well-deserved punishment."

Grandmamma could hardly believe this for she did

not think he looked such a bad boy; and there seemed no reason for him to destroy the chair. But to the uncle, Peter's confession only confirmed the suspicion which he had had from the beginning. The angry looks Peter had cast on Clara and the signs of resentment towards the newcomers to the Alm had not escaped the uncle. He had put two and two together and explained it all now to grandmamma. When he had finished, the lady said, "No, no, my dear Uncle, we don't want to punish the poor boy any more. One must be fair. We strangers have, for weeks, taken Heidi away from him, so he sits, day after day, and broods all by himself. No, no, we must be fair. Anger and resentment drove the boy to his revenge which was, perhaps, a little foolish; but we are all foolish when we are angry."

Grandmamma went over to Peter and sat down on the bench under the fir trees. In a kind voice she said, "Come, my boy, stand in front of me. I want to speak to you. Stop trembling and listen. You pushed the chair down the slope to destroy it; that was wicked and you knew that you deserved to be punished. So to avoid that you took a lot of trouble to hide the truth; but you see, he who does something wrong and thinks nobody will find out is always mistaken. God sees and hears everything and when He notices that somebody wants to hide a wrong deed He wakes up the little watchman whom He has placed inside us from our birth and who sleeps inside us until we do something wrong. This little watchman has a little prong in his hand and he prods us with it all the time so that we do not have a minute's peace. His voice torments us, too, for it keeps calling, 'Soon you will be found out! Now they'll come and drag you away!' So we live in terror and anxiety and never have a moment's happiness. Did you feel something like that, Peter?"

Peter nodded penitently, for that was exactly how he had felt.

"In still another way you miscalculated, for you wanted to do something wrong and something good came out of it. Because Clara had no chair and she wanted to see the beautiful flowers she tried hard to walk; and she succeeded, and in the end, was able to go every day to the pasture—much more frequently than she would have done in the chair. You see, Peter, God can turn evil into good for the one who was meant to be harmed; harm comes to the evil-doer instead. Do you understand, Peter? If so, don't forget; and if you ever again want to do something wrong, remember the little watchman inside with his prong and unpleasant voice, will you?"

"Yes, I will," answered Peter, still very depressed for he still did not know how the affair would end.

"Then everything is all right and the whole matter is settled," finished the grandmamma. "But now you shall have a souvenir from the Frankfurt visitors. Tell me, my boy, what would you like?"

Slowly Peter lifted his head and gazed at the grandmamma in astonishment.

He had expected some awful punishment and now he was being asked what he would like. He was completely confused.

"Yes, I am quite serious," continued the grandmamma. "You shall have something as a remembrance and as a token that the people from Frankfurt think no more than that you did something wrong. Do you understand, my boy?"

Now it began to dawn on Peter that he need not fear any punishment and that the kind lady had saved him from arrest by the police. It was a great weight off his mind. Now he saw too, that it was better to confess at once if one had done something wrong and suddenly he stammered, "And I also lost the paper."

The grandmamma had to think for a moment what this meant but soon she recalled the telegram and said kindly:

"That is right. Always confess at once what you have done and everything will be all right. And now have you any special wish?"

Peter felt quite giddy at the thought of being able to have anything he wanted. The annual fair at Maienfeld flashed before his eyes with all the beautiful things he had admired so often and never hoped to possess. There were the red whistles, which he could use for his goats; and the fascinating knives. Peter was deeply absorbed in his thoughts and he could not decide which of the two he would like the better. Suddenly he had a brainwave. "A penny," he said.

The grandmamma laughed. "That is not an extravagant wish," she said. "Come here!" She pulled out her purse and took from it four bright round shillings and on top of them she put four pennies. "Well, we want to settle our accounts," she said. "I will explain it to you. Here are just as many pennies as there are weeks in the year and so you will be able to spend a penny every week for a whole year."

"All my life?" asked Peter innocently.

Now the grandmamma could not help laughing heartily so that the gentlemen interrupted their talk to hear what was going on.

"Yes, my boy, that's a passage for my will," said the old lady. "I will put down, 'A penny a week to Peter as long as he lives.'" Herr Sesemann nodded his agreement and laughed too.

Peter looked once more at the present in his hand. He still could hardly believe his eyes. Then he said, "God bless you!" and off he went, running and leaping, all fear and anxiety gone.

After dinner, Clara took her father aside and said to him, "If you only knew, Papa, what the grandfather has done for me! I shall never forget it all my life. And I keep wondering, what could I give him or do for him, that would give him half the pleasure he has given me!"

"That is my dearest wish, too, my child," replied her father.

Herr Sesemann now went to the Alm-Uncle and seizing his hand, said, "My dear friend, let us have a word together. Believe me when I say that for years I have not known such happiness. Money and possessions have meant nothing to me since they have not helped to make my poor child well and happy. You have restored her health and given new life to her and me. Now, tell me, how can I show my gratitude? I can never repay what you have done, but whatever is in my power is at your disposal. Tell me, my friend, what can I do?"

The Alm-Uncle had listened in silence. Now he looked at Herr Sesemann and smiled. "Believe me, Herr Sesemann, I too am overjoyed at the girl's recovery on our Alm and my trouble has been well repaid by that. For your kind offer I thank you, but there is nothing I need; as long as I live I have enough for Heidi and myself. But if one wish only could be fulfilled I should have no more worries in this life."

"Speak, my dear friend," urged Herr Sesemann.

"I am old," continued the uncle, "and cannot expect to be here much longer. When I have passed away there will be nothing for the child and she has no relatives of any account. If you will promise that Heidi will never have to go out and earn her living among strangers then you will have amply repaid what I have done for your child."

"But there could never be any question about it!" exclaimed Herr Sesemann. "The child is one of us. Ask my mother and my daughter. They will never allow Heidi to go to strangers. This I promise you, both during my life and after, the child will never have to go among strangers. But she has made good friends, one of whom is our friend, the doctor. He is winding up his affairs and intends to come and settle here this autumn, in the Swiss mountains, for he has never felt so well and happy as in your and the child's company. You see, Heidi will now have two protectors. May they both live long!"

"God grant that will be so!" added the grandmamma and shook hands warmly with the Alm-Uncle. Then she embraced Heidi who stood beside her.

"And you, my dear Heidi, come, tell me, don't you have a particular wish?"

"Yes, certainly," replied Heidi, looking cheerfully up at the grandmamma.

"What is it child?" she encouraged.

"I would like my bed from Frankfurt with the three high pillows and the thick cover, so that Grandmother needn't lie with her head downhill and won't need to put her shawl on in bed any more because she is cold."

"My dear child, it is good you remind me to think of others in our happiness, those who are not so well off as we are. I will wire at once to Frankfurt. The bed will be here in two days and, with God's help, the grandmother will soon be sleeping comfortably in it."

Heidi skipped delightedly round the grandmamma. She wanted to go down at once and give the grandmother this happy message but the grandfather said reprovingly, "No, no, Heidi! When you have guests you can't run away like that!"

But the grandmamma supported Heidi, "My dear Uncle, we shall go together. We can then go on to Dorfli and send the wire off to Frankfurt. What do you think, my son?"

Until now, Herr Sesemann had not given much thought to his holiday plans. Originally, he had thought of taking a trip through Switzerland with his mother and had wondered if Clara would be fit to accompany them for part of the journey. But now he would be able to enjoy the company of his daughter more fully. He did not want to miss any of these beautiful days of late summer and decided to stay the night at Dorfli and the next morning to fetch Clara when all three would go to Ragatz and start their journey from there.

Clara was a little upset at the thought of leaving the Alm but there was so much to look forward to and so little time to think that she was soon quite cheerful again.

Brigitta was standing outside the cottage when the little company approached and she rushed inside quickly, crying, "They are coming, Mother!"

"Alas, it is true, then," sighed the grandmother. "Do you think they are taking the child with them? Did you see her?"

Presently the door flew open and Heidi rushed into the room, going at once to the Grandmother's corner and embracing her affectionately.

"Grandmother, Grandmother! My bed is coming from Frankfurt, and the three pillows and also the thick cover. It will be here in two days. Grandmamma has promised."

The grandmother smiled a little sadly, "What a kind lady she must be. I wish I could be happy that she is taking you with her, Heidi."

"What is all this? Who has been telling my good, old grandmother such tales?" said a kind voice. Grandmamma had overheard the conversation.

"No, no, that is out of the question! Heidi will stay

with the grandmother, but we will come back to the
Alm every year for we have good reason to thank God for
this spot, and especially for the miracle He has wrought
on our girl."

The grandmother's face lit up. Unable to speak, she
pressed Frau Sesemann's hand again and again, and two
large tears ran down her wrinkled cheeks.

Heidi clung affectionately to her and said, "Hasn't
it all happened as in the hymn I read to you? When the
bed comes from Frankfurt you will be much better too,
Grandmother."

"Ah, yes, Heidi. God has sent me so many good
things. Is it possible that there are such kind people
who trouble themselves about a poor old woman?"

"My good Grandmother," interrupted Frau Sesemann,
"in the eyes of God we are all equally poor and need His
help; and He does not forget us. We must say good-bye
now, but only until we meet again next year, and we
certainly never will forget the dear grandmother."

Frau Sesemann took the grandmother's hand again,
and with the old woman's blessing, Herr Sesemann
and his mother continued their journey down into the
valley.

Next morning, Clara was very sad about leaving the
Alm where she had been so happy; but Heidi did her
best to comfort her. "Summer will soon come again, and
then it will be better still, for you are well now and we
can go every day with the goats up to the pastures."

Clara dried her tears, "Don't forget to remember
me to Peter and the goats," she said.

Herr Sesemann had arrived and was beckoning to the
children, for it was time to go. Heidi stood at the very
edge of the slope and waved to Clara until she disappeared
from sight.

Frau Sesemann did not forget how cold it could be

in winter on the mountain. She sent a big parcel to Goat Peter's hut; it contained warm clothing of every description so that the grandmother would never again have to sit trembling with cold.

The doctor arrived in Dorfli, and, on the Alm-Uncle's advice, he bought the house where the old man and Heidi stayed during the winter. The doctor decided to have it rebuilt, part of it for himself and the other part for the uncle and Heidi for their winter lodgings.

As the days went by, the doctor and the Alm-Uncle became very good friends and often their conversation would turn to Heidi because, for both of them, it was the greatest joy to have the child with them in their new house.

One day, when the doctor and the uncle were standing together, seeing how the new building was getting on, the doctor said to the old man; "I share your happiness in the child and I feel I am the nearest to her after you; so I want to share also the responsibilities and to provide for her as best I can, so that I may hope that in my old age she will stay with me. That is my greatest wish, that Heidi should have the same claims on me as though she were my own child. Then we will be able to leave her free of worries when you and I have departed."

The grandfather pressed the doctor's hand and the doctor could read in the eyes of his friend how greatly touched he was by these words.

At this moment Heidi and Peter were sitting with the grandmother. Heidi had such a story to tell them that she hardly took time to breathe. They had seen very little of each other during the summer, and how much had happened!

It was difficult to tell which of the three radiant faces shone most happily.

Brigitta, with Heidi's help, at last understood the

story of Peter's miraculous weekly penny and her face beamed, perhaps most radiantly of all.

At last, the grandmother said to Heidi, "Read one of the hymns to me, child! I want to thank our Heavenly Father for all the mercy He has bestowed on us!"

THE END

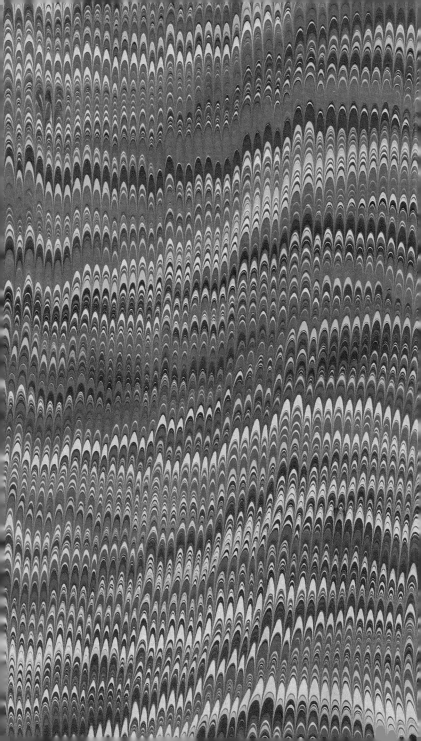